American Mandolin Method

VOLUME 1

Brian Wicklund and Ben Winship

Online Audio www.melbay.com/20145BCDEB

Audio Contents

1	Boil 'em Cabbage Down	16	Amazing Grace
2	Shortnin' Bread	17	Red River Valley
3	Little Liza Jane	18	Shady Grove
4	Camptown Races	19	Sugar Hill
5	Cripple Creek	20	Cluck Old Hen
6	Buffalo Gals	21	Arran Boat Song
7	Angeline Baker	22	Over the Waterfall
8	Old Joe Clark	23	Si Beag Si Mor
9	Cindy	24	Sandy Boys
10	Crawdad Song	25	Southwind
11	Bonaparte's Retreat	26	Red Wing
12	Red Haired Boy	27	Cairo
13	Country Waltz	28	Miss McLeod's Reel
14	Girl I Left Behind Me	29	Turkey in the Straw
15	Down in the Valley	30	Stinky's Blues

1 2 3 4 5 6 7 8 9 0

Visit us on the Web at www.melbay.com — E-mail us at email@melbay.com

About the Authors

Brian Wicklund was seven years old when his mother thought he should take Suzuki violin lessons. He was surprised to find out that he liked it. When he heard bluegrass music for the first time as a third grader, however, he really flipped out. Brian practiced hard and got to be pretty good. As a pimply teen, some of the prize money from the fiddle contests he won went towards purchasing his first mandolin. He liked that it was like a violin but could be played in the backseat of a car or lying in a bed. After graduating from Gustavus Adolphus College with a degree in elementary education, he promptly started playing and teaching fiddle and mandolin full time. Brian currently keeps a busy schedule teaching fiddle and mandolin lessons, workshops and camps including his Fiddle Pal Camps across the US, Canada, Sweden and UK. He is a sought–after studio musician and regularly performs with his band *The Barley Jacks* and with good buddy and co-author Ben Winship in *Brother Mule*. He has toured Japan, Canada, UK, and Europe and nearly every state in the US. Find out about Brian's recordings, performances and workshops at www.fiddlepal.com

photo courtesy of Glenn Oakley

Ben Winship is a self–taught musician who has been playing mandolin for over 30 years. He is a versatile player who is comfortable with a wide range of styles from bluegrass and old-time, to Dixieland and blues. On stage Ben can most often be found playing along side co-author Brian Wicklund in *Brother Mule* or with the *Growling Old Men*. Over the past 25 years, gigs have taken him everywhere from Hawaii to Shetland, Anchorage to Ecuador, with appearances along the way at places like the Telluride Bluegrass Festival, A Prairie Home Companion, NYC's Bottom Line and the Vancouver Folk Festival. In addition to playing the mandolin, Ben is also a well–respected multi instrumentalist, singer and songwriter. Tim O'Brien refers to him as "one of the acoustic music scene's best writers." When not performing, he can be found in his studio producing CDs, recording his own music and teaching. www.benwinship.com.

About the Artist

Brian Barber is pretty tall and has been illustrating and designing for many publications and for advertising agencies in Minneapolis since 1989. He moved to Minneapolis from Nebraska, where he attended the University of Nebraska-Lincoln. His musical experience includes playing drums and guitar in several rock and roll bands. Although new to the mandolin, he is experienced with the fiddle from when he was once fighting with his little sister and broke her bow. He got into really big trouble. I'm sure if she had been playing mandolin he would have broken that too. Brian's other illustrations are at www.brianbarber.com.

Foreword

For the past several decades the mandolin has become increasingly popular in acoustic music. Tuned like a violin, the mandolin came with European immigrants to America. Its versatility as both a solo and ensemble instrument across a broad range of genres has assured the mandolin a permanent place in American music.

During the turn of the 20th century, mandolin orchestras were popular throughout the country playing Vaudeville and classical music. Beginning in the 1930s, Bill Monroe made the mandolin an integral part of his bluegrass music. These days there are a number of players such as Chris Thile, Sam Bush, David Grisman and Mike Marshall who have been expanding the boundaries of mandolin music. It's a really exciting time to be a mandolin player!

The American Mandolin Method, Volume 1 was written for beginner students. You will have fun using the first ten simple tunes to learn right and left hand positions and fundamental picking techniques. Then you will progress to the next batch of eighth note based tunes which emphasize pick direction. After exploring tremolo in the next section, you will incorporate all of the techniques in the dozen classic tunes that follow.

We have taken great care to present each tune in what we believe to be its basic melody in its most common key. Because many of these tunes are passed down via the oral tradition, they can change from one generation to the next or from one part of the country to another. However, one who learns the melodies in this book should have no problem playing with folk musicians anywhere.

We personally get the most enjoyment from playing music when "jamming" with others. To help students develop ensemble skills, we have included the chords and lyrics to the songs. The majority of the tunes in this book can also be found in *The American Fiddle Method* books for fiddle, cello, viola and piano accompaniment. They are presented in the same keys so that mandolin players, fiddlers, cellists and piano players will all be able to jam together.

Finally, we felt it was important to include a listening/play-along audio that captures the excitement of playing these tunes. Mandolin players will enjoy listening, playing and singing along with the fine musicians on the accompanying recording.

–Brian and Ben

Table of Contents

How to Become a Great Mandolin Player

1. **Listen to the recording that accompanies this book.** Listening to the recording will familiarize you with the melodies, good intonation, tone and style of the music. Listen anytime: while you eat, when you are riding in the car, or as you go to sleep at night. The more you listen, the faster and easier it will be to learn the tunes. Listen to as many other mandolin recordings as you can, too.

2. **Practice regularly.** Practice four to seven times a week, between 30 minutes and two hours each time. For the first portion of your practice, warm up with simple exercises and scales to get your fingers moving, then tackle whatever new material you are working on. Finish your practice with a review of old tunes by playing along with the recording.

Make sessions the same time and place every day to establish a habit. Some people like to keep track of their practices on a calendar and then give themselves a reward for a certain number of practices. We suggest a reward such as a new mandolin recording or tickets to a concert.

3. **Practice smart.** This element of practice is often overlooked! You can learn skills much faster if you understand the basic principles of learning and memory. There are two levels of knowing how to play a tune: **melodic memory** and **muscle memory**. After repeatedly listening to the audio, you will be able to hum the tunes and probably pick out the notes on your mandolin with or without the notation. You will be able to hear what the next note should sound like before you play it. This is an important first step in learning the tune. However, in order to be able to play the tune at jamming tempo without making mistakes, you need to take the next step of committing the tune to muscle memory.

When you have done a skill enough times, your brain and muscles get used to that skill and it becomes a habit. Muscle memory allows us to successfully complete a physical task 'automatically'— without having to concentrate on its every single detail. That's why we can walk and talk at the same time, bounce a basketball while thinking about our next move, or play a tune at break-neck speed while concentrating on playing expressively. Good players are not just satisfied with their brains knowing how a tune goes; they make sure their muscles know too!

Because your muscles "learn" whatever actions they repeat, it is very important to be sure that you are learning the music correctly and that you are using good position, tone and technique. Your muscles learn an incorrect skill as readily as a correct one, so make sure you are repeating exactly what you want your muscles to memorize. Everybody knows how difficult it is to break a bad habit!

When learning a new tune, follow these steps:

1. After you have listened to the audio, pick through the melody, either by ear or by reading the notation.
2. Slowly play a small part of the beginning of the tune. If you make a mistake, remember the note that came *before* the mistake.
3. Play the phrase again and pause on the note before your mistake, think about the correct note that comes next and play it.
4. Repeat the phrase until you consistently play it correctly.
5. Start from the beginning of the tune, and play through the next phrase. Apply the same learning steps to this phrase as you did to the first. When you can play the first and second phrases together without error, begin working on the third phrase, and then the fourth, until you can play them all without error. Then work on playing the tune up to speed while concentrating on good position, tone, and technique.

4. **Jam with other musicians.** After you have memorized your tunes and can play them at the speed of the recording, you are ready to jam. This is your reward for all of your hard work. Join a local bluegrass or folk music society that sponsors regular jams. Go to music festivals and open mics. Don't be shy about meeting people and asking them to jam or to show you a lick or two. Some of these meetings will turn into lasting friendships and regular jam opportunities.

Parts of a Mandolin

F Style

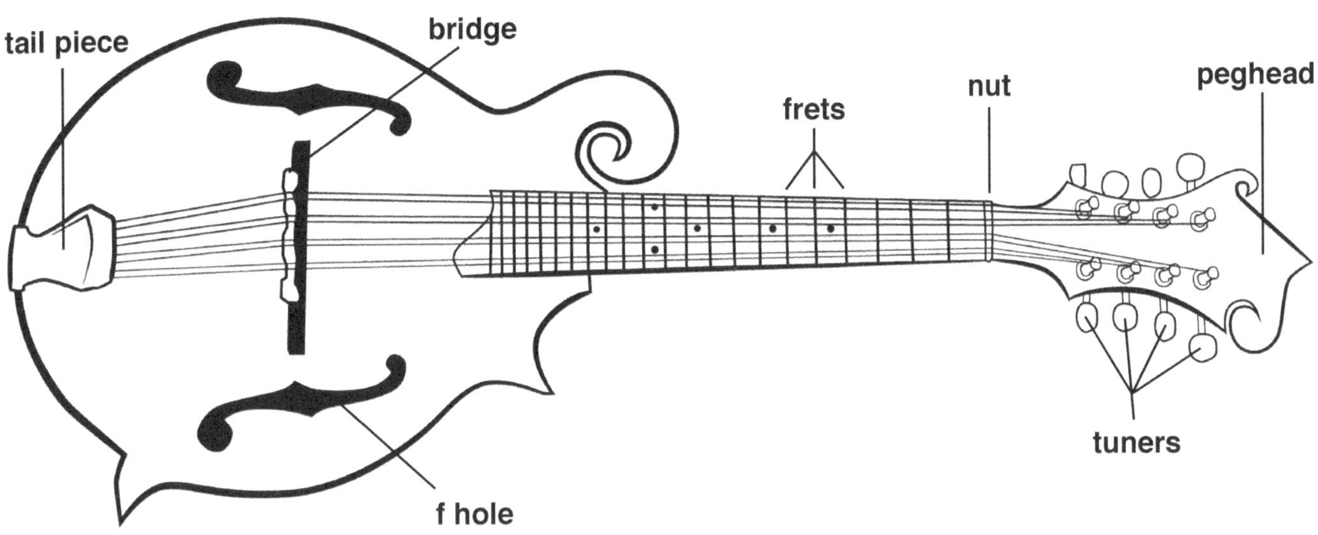

A Style

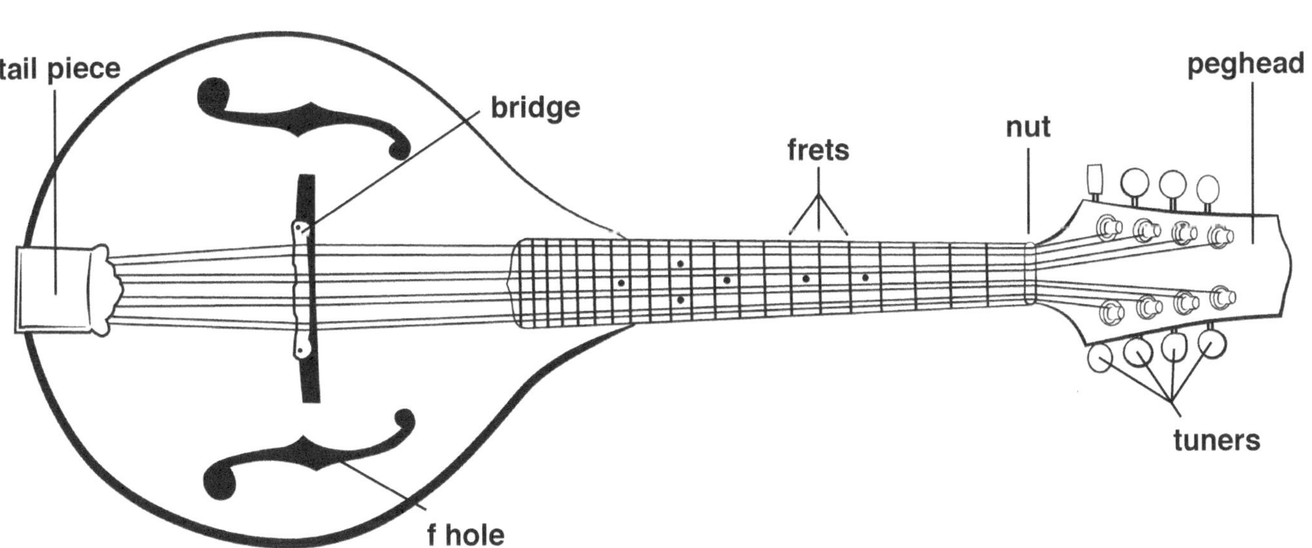

Tuning the Mandolin

Mandolin strings are tuned to G, D, A, E in pairs from low to high. The diagram below shows the pitches relative to a piano keyboard. For beginning students, we recommend using an electronic tuner. Electronic tuners that clip on to the peghead are inexpensive and easy to use. Note: when tuning the mandolin, it is more effective to start slightly below the pitch and tighten the string as you raise the pitch.

Always make sure you pluck the string and let it ring whenever adjusting the pitch. If you can't hear the string ring when you are making an adjustment, you may over tighten the string or unknowingly twist the wrong tuner and break the string.

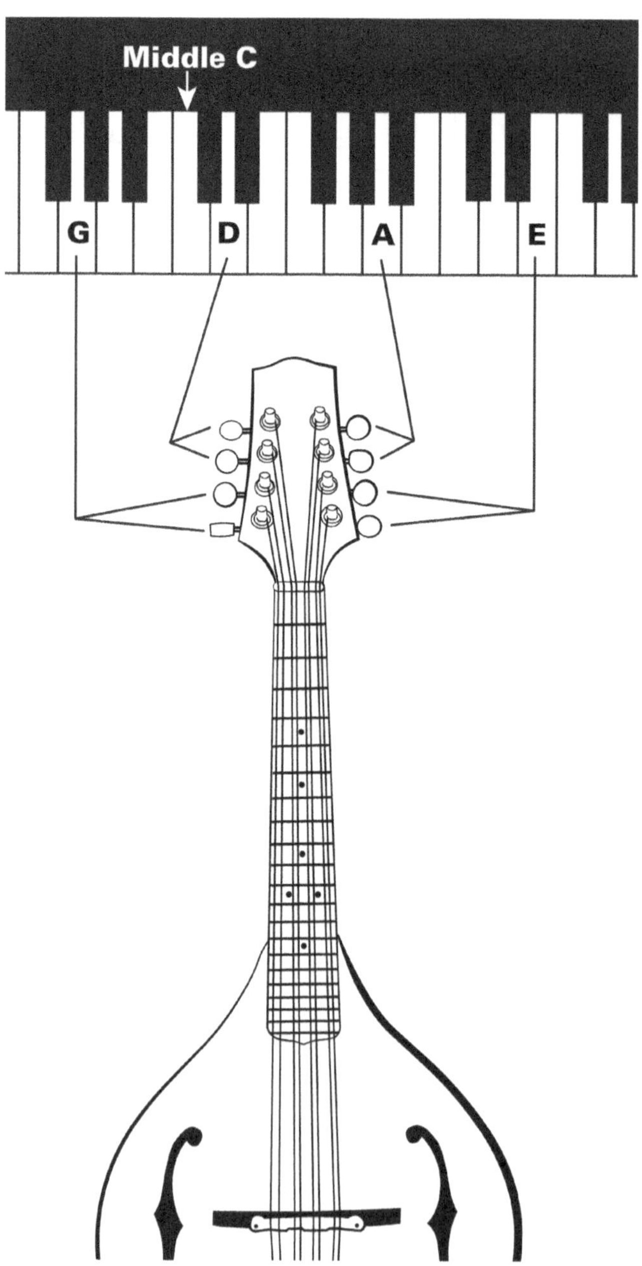

Mandolin Position

Adjusting the Strap

Although there are players who don't use a strap, most do. Most players like Ben prefer to put their right arm, shoulder and head through the strap (fig. 1). Other players like Brian wear the strap hanging from their right shoulder with only their arm through (fig. 2). You might try both ways to see which feels the most comfortable and secure. It is a good idea to get in the habit of wearing your strap whether you are standing or sitting down to play.

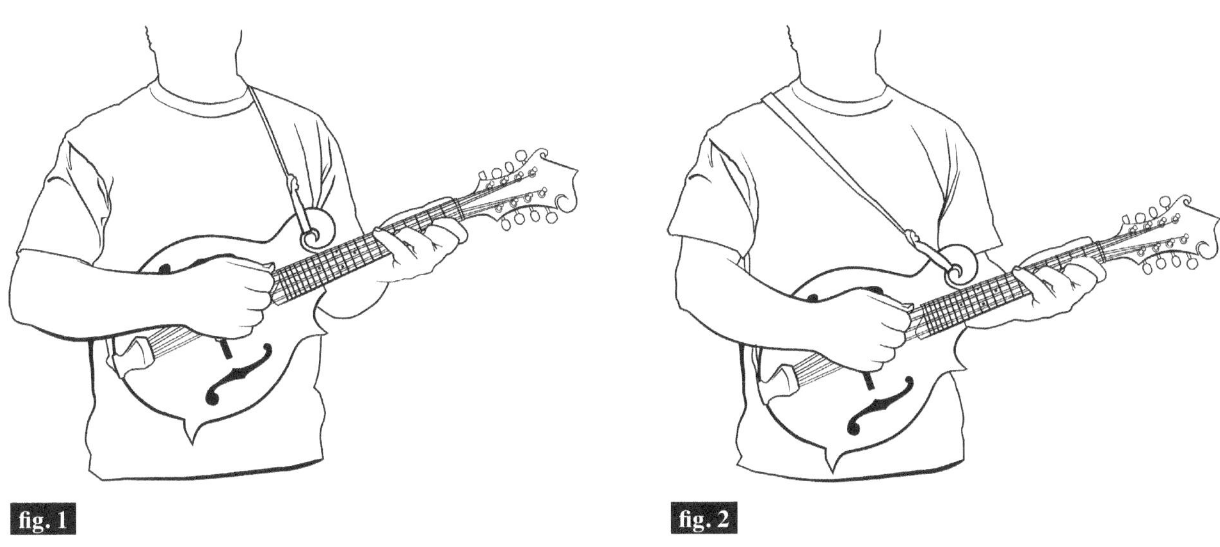

fig. 1

fig. 2

To adjust the strap sit in an armless upright chair, rest the mandolin on your right thigh and lean it against your body. Observe the distance from your shoulders to the mandolin. Then tighten up the slack in your strap so that when you stand up, the mandolin remains the same position as it was when you were sitting. Be careful that no belt buckles, hard buttons or zippers scratch the back of the mandolin.

Position Checklist

Holding the mandolin correctly will help you get the best sound and maximize playing dexterity with the least amount of effort.

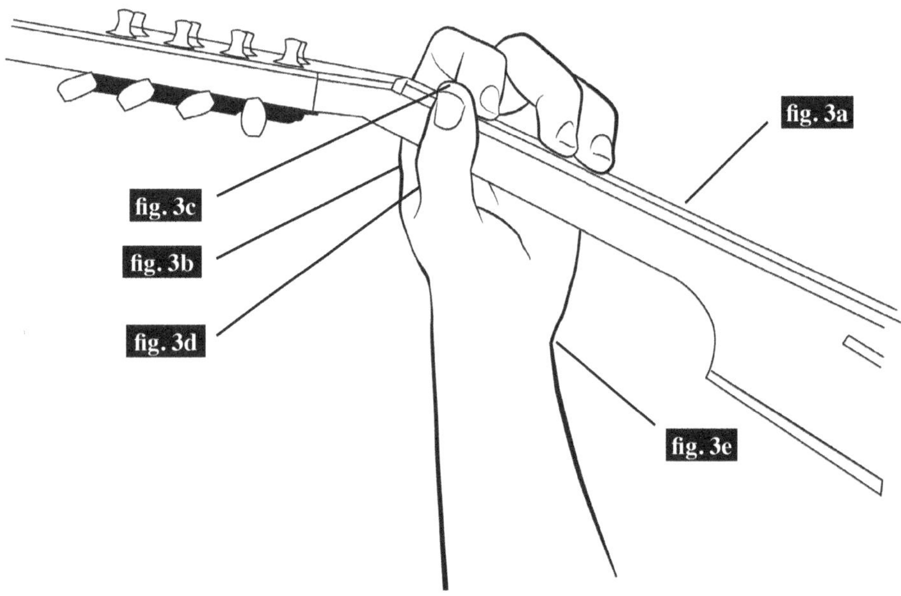

- The mandolin neck should be raised at a slight angle to the floor. (fig. 1 and 2)
- Your view of the fingerboard will be vertical (fig. 3a). Resist the temptation to lay the mandolin flat on your lap or crane your neck to look over it.
- The mandolin neck should rest between the middle joint of the thumb and where your index finger joins your hand (fig. 3b).
- The tip of your thumb should protrude over the edge of the fret board. (fig. 3c)
- There should be a small gap at the crook of your thumb. (fig. 3d)
- Your wrist should be straight. (fig. 3e)
- Your elbow should hang loosely and relaxed at your side.

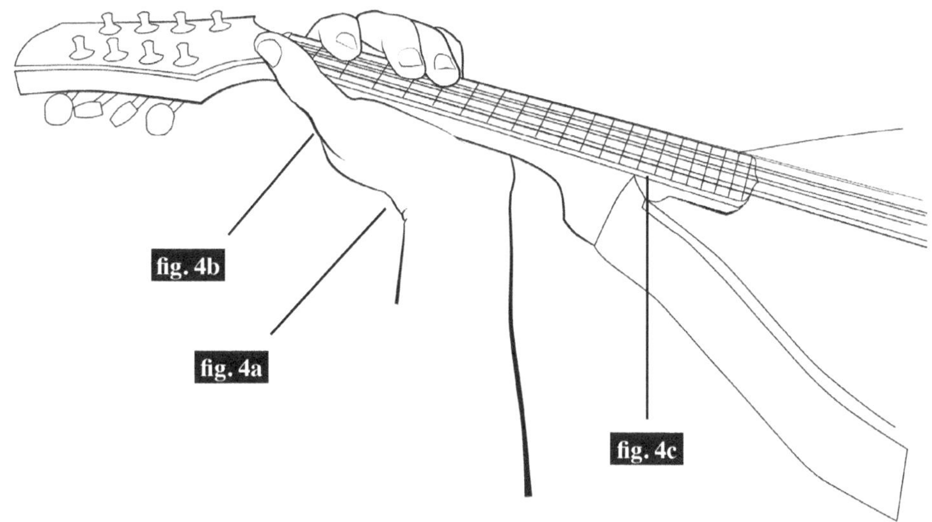

Common mistakes

- Neck pointing up too high.
- Wrist bent (fig. 4a).
- Neck sits in crook of thumb (fig. 4b).
- Left elbow sticks out.
- Leaning the mandolin back too far to look over the fingerboard (fig. 4c).

Picking Technique

There are many different looking (and sounding) right-hand techniques. Good picking technique allows for the most dexterity and richest tone with the least amount of effort.

Pick Choice

There are many different pick shapes, materials, textures, thicknesses and colors. Picks are made from plastic, nylon, tortoise shell (not recommended as some tortoise species are endangered), bone, horn or even a wild–colored plastic called "clown barf." Probably the most common choice for beginning mandolin players is a teardrop shaped, medium to heavy gauge pick.

The main factors that influence tone and playability in picks are thickness and shape. Generally, thinner picks are brighter sounding and thicker picks are darker sounding. The thickness of picks is measured in millimeters. Medium-gauge picks (in the .70-1.00 mm range) are a good thickness for beginners. Light-gauge picks have a "thwappy" sound and a slow response and are therefore not recommended. Thicker picks (in the 1.2 – 2 mm range) generate a fuller tone that many players like, but they can be a little more difficult to use for beginners.

The shape of the points influence the tone and playability of a pick as well. Pointy picks sound brighter and rounded picks sound darker. Pointy picks tend to be easier to use for beginners.

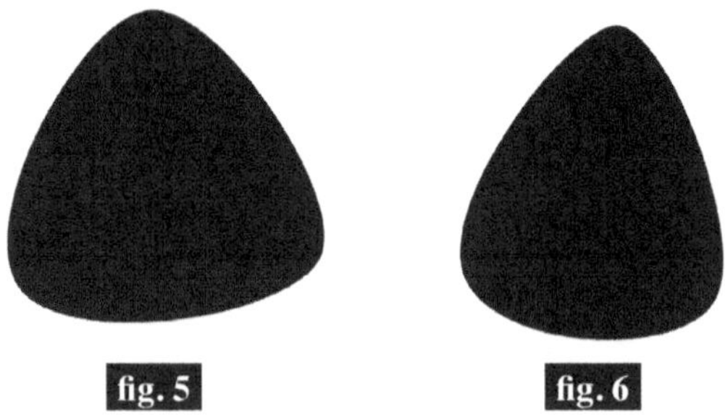
fig. 5 fig. 6

The two most common pick shapes are triangular (fig. 5) and teardrop (fig. 6). You will want to experiment and see which feels most comfortable.

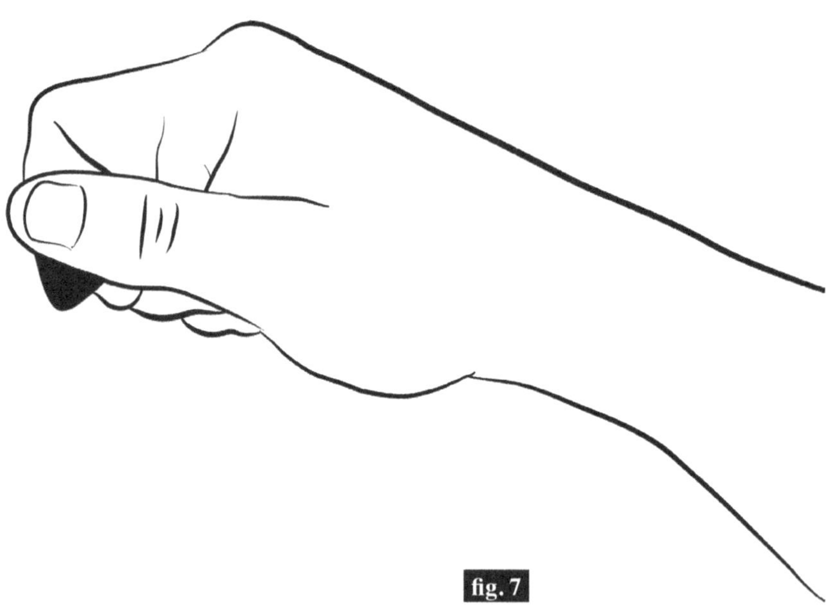
fig. 7

Holding the Pick

- Most players hold the pick between the thumb and side of the index finger.
- Curl the fingers of your right hand into a very loose fist.
- Rest the pick on the last joint of your index finger and gently squeeze the pick with the pad of your thumb. Your thumb will be straight but not "locked."
- The pick's point should extend roughly one-quarter inch past your index finger.
- Your hold on the pick should be relaxed not clenched. It will be just strong enough to keep the pick rigid as you play through the strings.

Positioning the Pick Hand

Having a point of contact for your hand on the mandolin makes it easier to consistently pick the strings accurately. Most mandolin players rest the base of their palm *lightly* on the bridge.

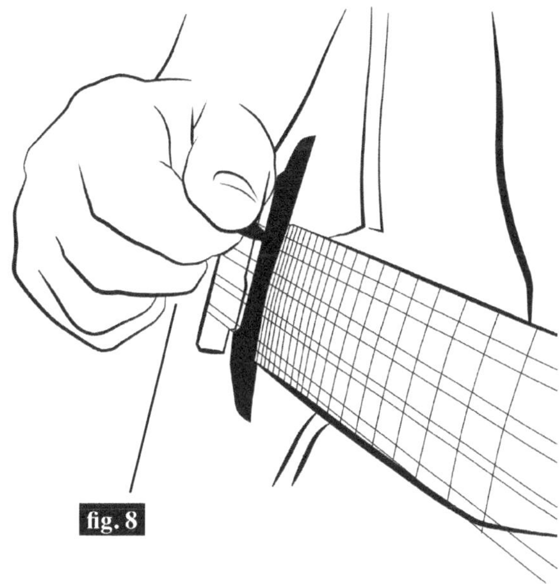
fig. 8

- The point of contact is the muscle at the base of the thumb which acts as a pivot point during picking.
- There will be a gap between the bridge and the pinky side of your palm (fig. 8)
- Keep the fingers of your right hand loosely curled inwards. This will keep them "out of the way" and will help you resist the temptation to plant them on the top of your mandolin.

The Sweet Spot

The "sweet spot" on the mandolin is the spot on the string which has the both the richest tone and the greatest volume. Experiment by picking close to the bridge. Notice that the tone is loud but very bright and brittle. Now pick over the fret board and notice the tone is warm but quiet. The sweet spot, which is both warm and loud, is located near or over the end of the fingerboard, about 3 to 3 ½ inches from the bridge. To reach the sweet spot while resting the thumb side of your palm on the bridge means that your thumb will be nearly fully extended. The meaty part of the base of your thumb may touch the G string. This isn't a problem until you play the G string. To play the G string without muting it with your hand, shift your hand up slightly to rest on the corner of the bridge.

Picking Motion

- The picking motion is mostly from the wrist (with a little help from the forearm). The fingers of the pick hand don't really move much.
- The motion of the pick should be perpendicular to the strings.
- Dig in enough to produce a clear full tone while keeping your pick hand relaxed.
- Each time you pick, you should ring both strings in the pair. The ringing of both strings together gives the mandolin it's distinctive sound. Watch the strings when you pick up and down and make sure you can see both strings in the pair vibrating. A common mistake for beginners is to pick the top string of the pair on the down stroke and the bottom string of the pair on the upstroke.

Fingering Technique

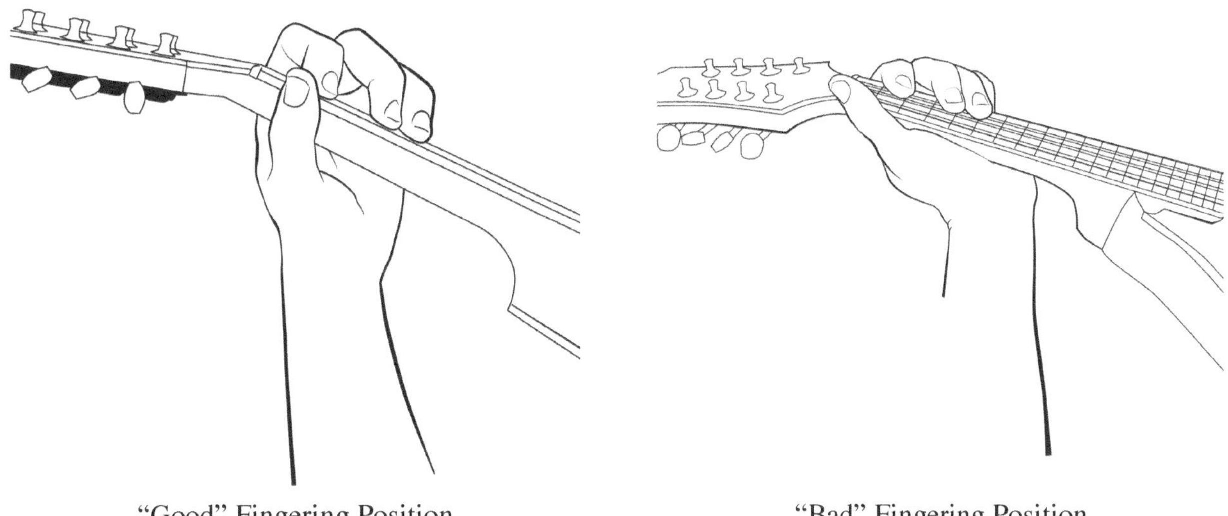

"Good" Fingering Position

"Bad" Fingering Position

- Make sure you push down the string with your fingertips, not the pads.
- Create clean tone by placing your fingertips just behind the frets. If the fingertip is too far from the fret or on top of the fret, the tone becomes muffled or buzzy.
- Keep all your fingers close to the fret board so they are ready and waiting. It is a common mistake of beginners to let the fingers drift away from the fret board and straighten when they are not in use. *(Tip: The key is to watch your third finger and never let it get farther than one–half inch above the fifth fret. If your third finger hovers there, your first and second fingers will too. Don't worry about your fourth finger, it may have a mind of its own.)*

Tablature and Standard Notation

The music in this book is presented in both standard notation and tablature (tab). Tab is a simple method of notation that describes which string and fret to use (if you already know how to read standard notation, then you shouldn't need tab).

Unless specifically noted, use your first finger (index) to play frets 1 and 2; second finger (middle) to play frets 3 and 4; third finger (ring) to play frets 5 and 6; and fourth finger (pinky) to play fret 7.

Each line represents a pair of strings and each number tells you which fret to play. For example, the tab below tells you to play following order of notes:

4th fret of the G string (second finger)
5th fret of D (third finger)
2nd fret of the A string (first finger)
5th fret of A string (third finger)
3rd fret of E string (second finger)

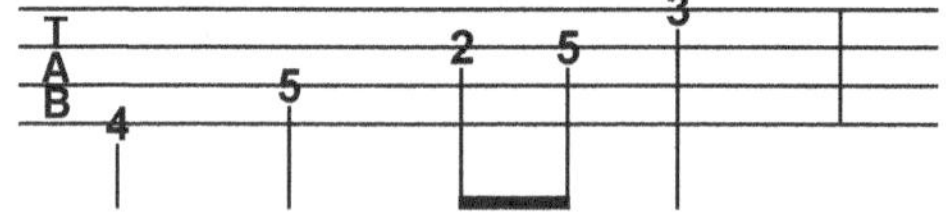

Pick Direction and Rhythm

Proper pick direction is essential to good mandolin playing and is critical to playing at faster tempos and with correct phrasing. The concept is simple:

> ***Play down strokes on notes that land on beats 1, 2, 3 and 4.***
> ***Play up strokes on the eighth notes that land between the beats.***

In the example below, all of the notes in the measures land on downbeats (beats 1, 2, 3, 4) and are played with down strokes. *(Tip: You will learn this fastest if you synchronize your pick direction with tapping your foot.)*

If you have a metronome, set it at a tempo of 80 beats per minute (BPM). Play the following measures while doing these three things at once:

1. Tap your foot.
2. Count "one, two, three, four."
3. Pick down on each beat.

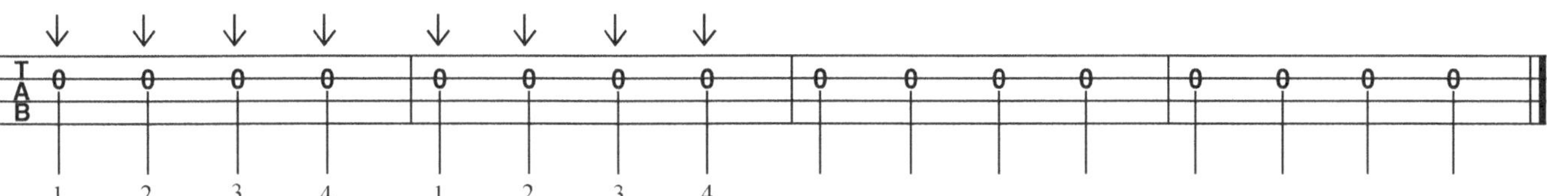

Think of your pick as being connected to your tapping foot with an imaginary rod. *Your pick and foot move down and up together*.

Now let's add eighth notes. With your metronome, set it at 80 BPM, play the following measures while doing these three things at once:

1. Tap your foot.
2. Count "one, *and*, two, *and*, three, *and*, four, *and*."
3. Pick down on each beat, and up stroke on the "*ands*."

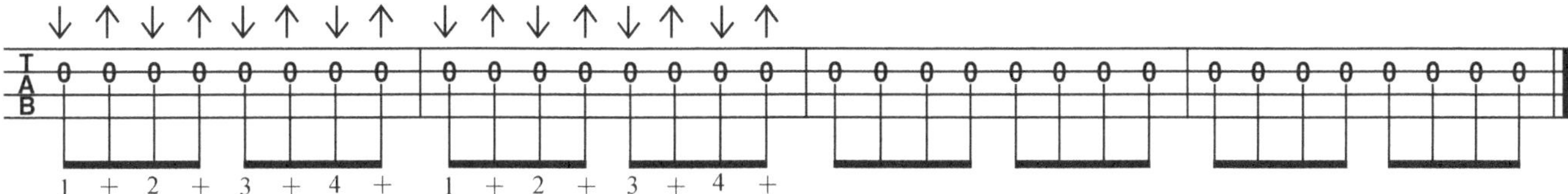

Continue to think of your pick as being connected to your tapping foot with an imaginary rod. *Your pick and foot move down and up together*. Strive to make your up strokes as strong and full as your down strokes.

Think of your right hand as a little machine. Once it starts moving down and up in steady time, it doesn't stop until the end of the tune. However, you won't necessarily sound a note with each downward or upward movement of your hand! There are an infinite number of rhythmic patterns that include combinations of quarter notes, eighth notes, rests and more. You'll play these rhythms while your pick hand constantly moves up and down with your foot. Think back to the first exercise we played, when you were playing only down strokes. Even though you were sounding only down strokes, your hand was moving up on the "ands."

In the exercises below, keep your hand in steady motion and in synch with your foot. This will ensure that you play all of the down strokes and up strokes in the correct places. *Tap your foot with your down strokes.*

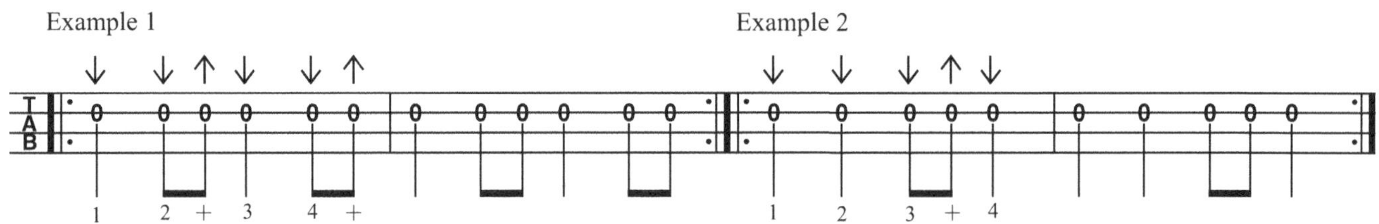

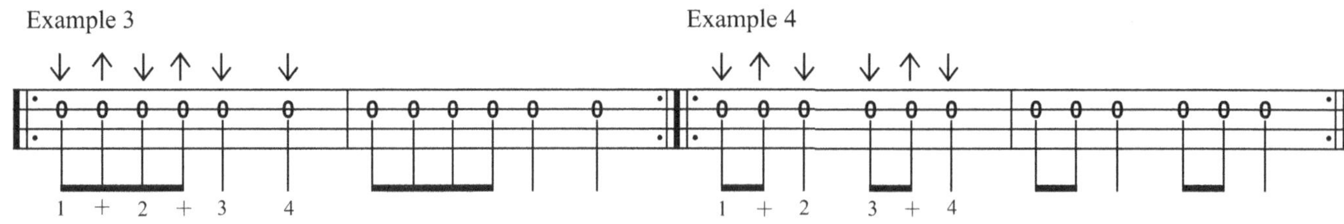

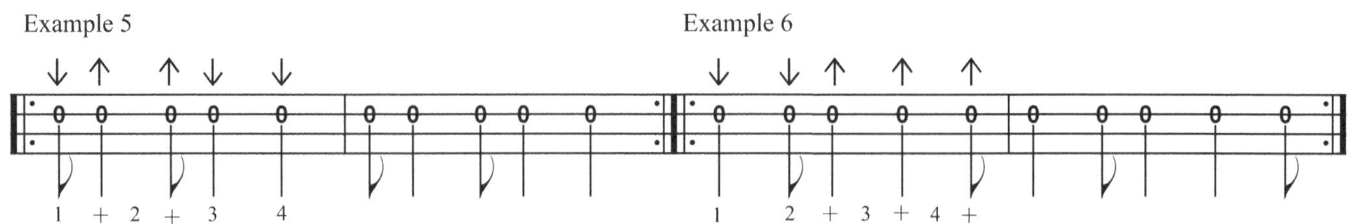

Crossing Strings

Maintaining the correct pick direction while crossing from one string to another can be tricky for the beginner. Remember that pick direction is determined *entirely* by the rhythm of the song and *has nothing to do with* the relative location of the string you are going to or coming from. Intuition might suggest that when you are crossing from the A string to the E string (a string that is physically lower) you would use a down stroke, or when crossing from the A string to the D string (a string that is physically above) that you would use an up stroke. However, the location of the strings is irrelevant. *The only thing that determines pick direction is rhythm.*

The following exercises are rhythm patterns with a mix of string crossings. Tap your foot and synchronize it with your pick direction.

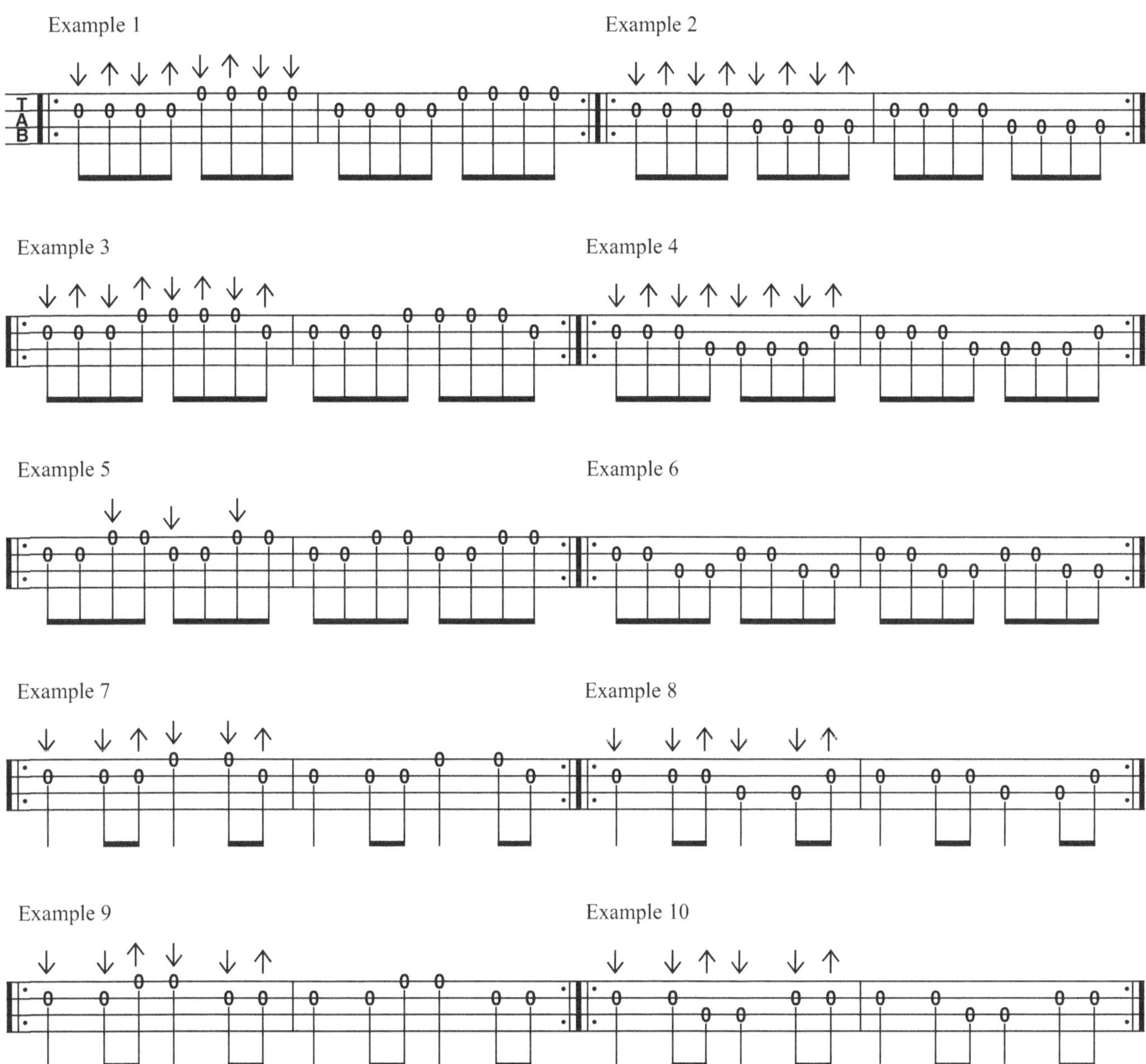

Note: As you speed up, you'll probably find tapping your foot on all four beats to be fatiguing. That's why most players tap their foot on only the first and third beats. However, make sure you have mastered the pick direction technique with tapping on all four beats before you switch to only tapping on the first and third beats.

Scales

Before we move on to the tunes, let's learn some scales. While there are many different types of scales, we'll start with the two-octave G and A major scales. Use them as a warm-up, paying close attention to coordinating your right and left hand movements, getting good tone and alternating down strokes and up strokes.

Two Octave G Major Scale

Two Octave A Major Scale

Boil 'em Cabbage Down

This tune was first performed in minstel shows before the American Civil War.
"Hoe cake" is bread that slaves baked on garden hoes over an open fire.
The first version is all down strokes. Pay close attention to your pick direction on the rhythm variation.

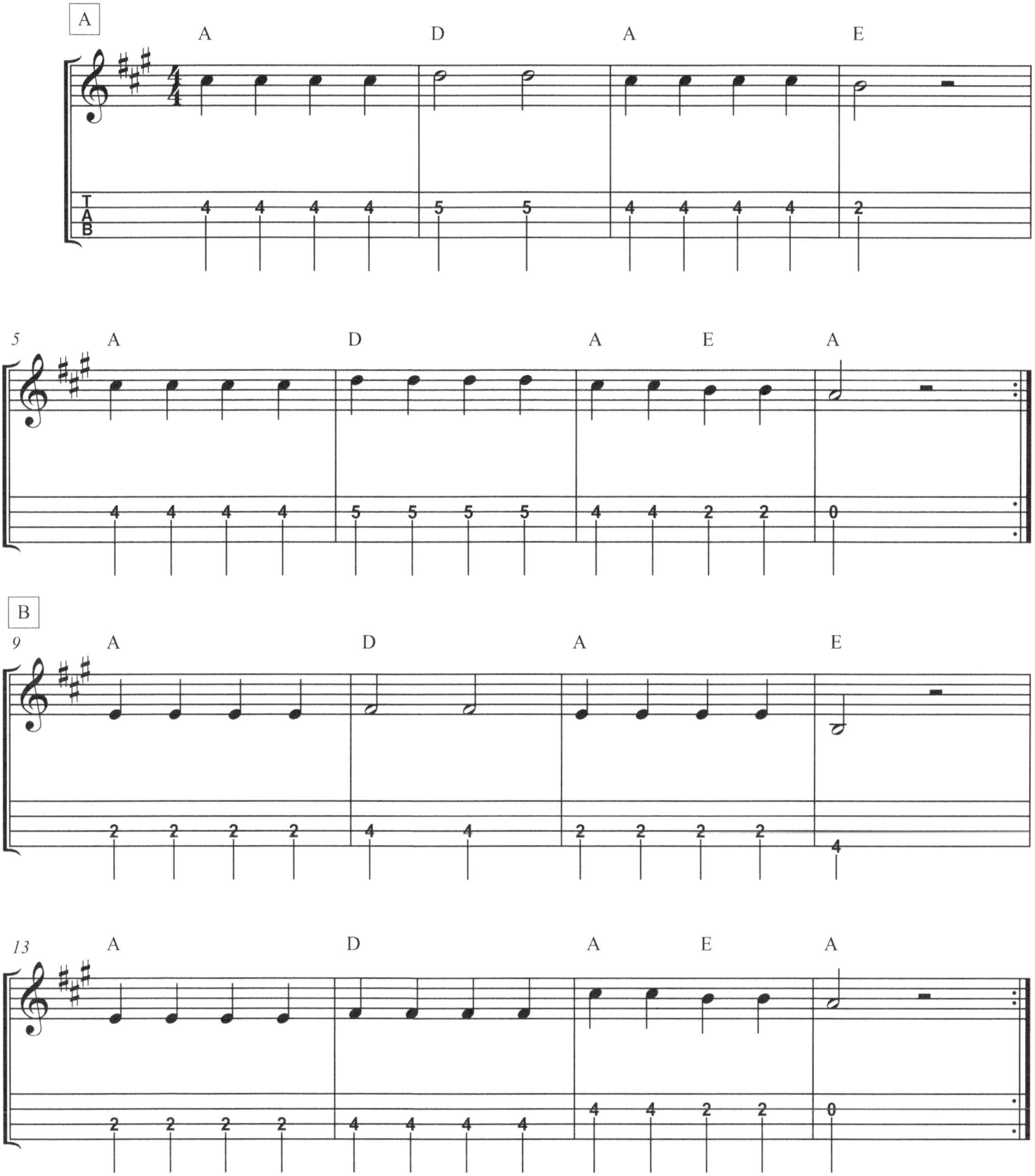

A

A D A E

5 A D A E A

B

9 A D A E

13 A D A E A

(verses and chorus sung to A part)

1. Went up on the mountain to give my horn a blow
Thought I heard my true love say, "Yonder stands my beau"
Raccoon and a 'possum running side by side
Raccoon asked the 'possum, "Won't you be my bride?"

Chorus

Boil 'em cabbage down boys, turn, turn the hoe cake brown
The only song that I can sing is boil 'em cabbage down

2. Raccoon up a 'simmon tree, 'possum on the ground
Raccoon said to the 'possum, "Shake them 'simmons down"
Jay bird died with the whooping cough, sparrow died with the colic
Along came a frog with a fiddle on his back,
inquiring his way to the frolic

3. Took my dog to the blacksmith's shop to have his mouth made small
He turned around a time or two, and swallowed the shop and all

Shortnin' Bread

This is a traditional African-American song.

Rhythm Variation

1. Three little children lyin' in a bed
   Two was sick and one nearly dead
   Sent for the doctor, the doctor said
   "Feed those children on shortnin' bread"

Chorus
Momma's little baby loves shortnin', shortnin'
Momma's little baby loves shortnin' bread
Momma's little baby loves shortnin', shortnin'
Momma's little baby loves shortnin' bread

2. Put on the skillet, put on the lid
   Momma gonna bake a little shortnin' bread
   That ain't all she's gonna do
   Momma gonna make a little coffee, too

3. I slip to the kitchen, lift up the lid
   Filled my pocket full of shortnin' bread
   Stole the skillet, stole the lid
   Stole the gal makin' shortnin' bread

4. Caught me with the skillet, they caught me with the lid
   They caught me with the gal makin' shortnin' bread
   Six dollars for the skillet, six dollars for the lid
   And six months in jail eatin' shortnin' bread

Little Liza Jane

With a history dating back at least to the early 1900s,
this one has become a standard in folk, traditional jazz, and bluegrass.

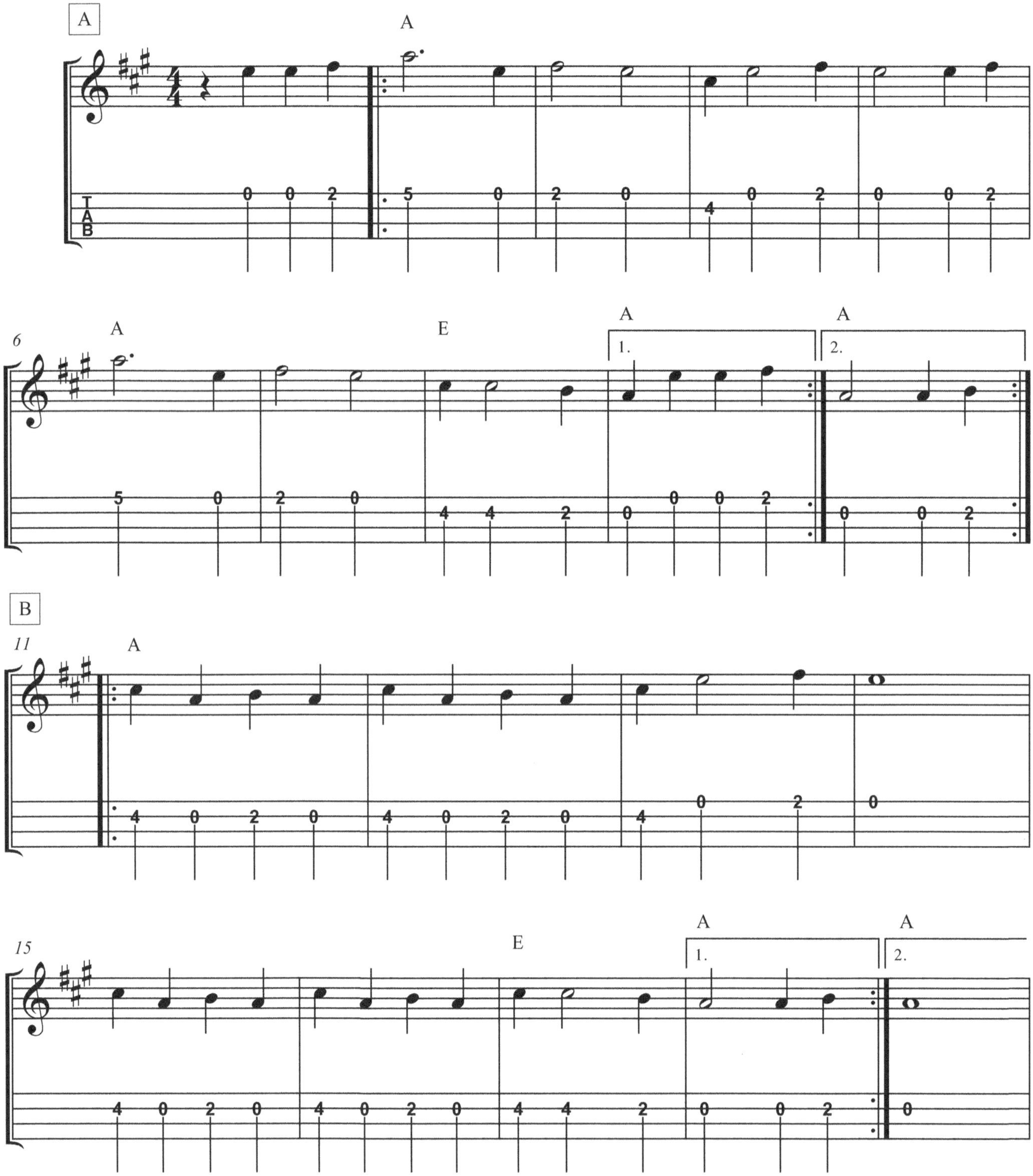

1. I got a house in Baltimore, Little Liza Jane
   Street cars running by my door, Little Liza Jane

Chorus
Oh, Eliza, Little Liza Jane
Oh, Eliza, Little Liza Jane

2. I wish I had a candy box to put my sweetheart in
   I'd take her out and kiss her twice and put her right back in

3. I've got a gal and you've got none, Little Liza Jane
   I've got a gal that calls me "hun", Little Liza Jane

Camptown Races

Stephen Foster wrote this song about horse racing in 1850.

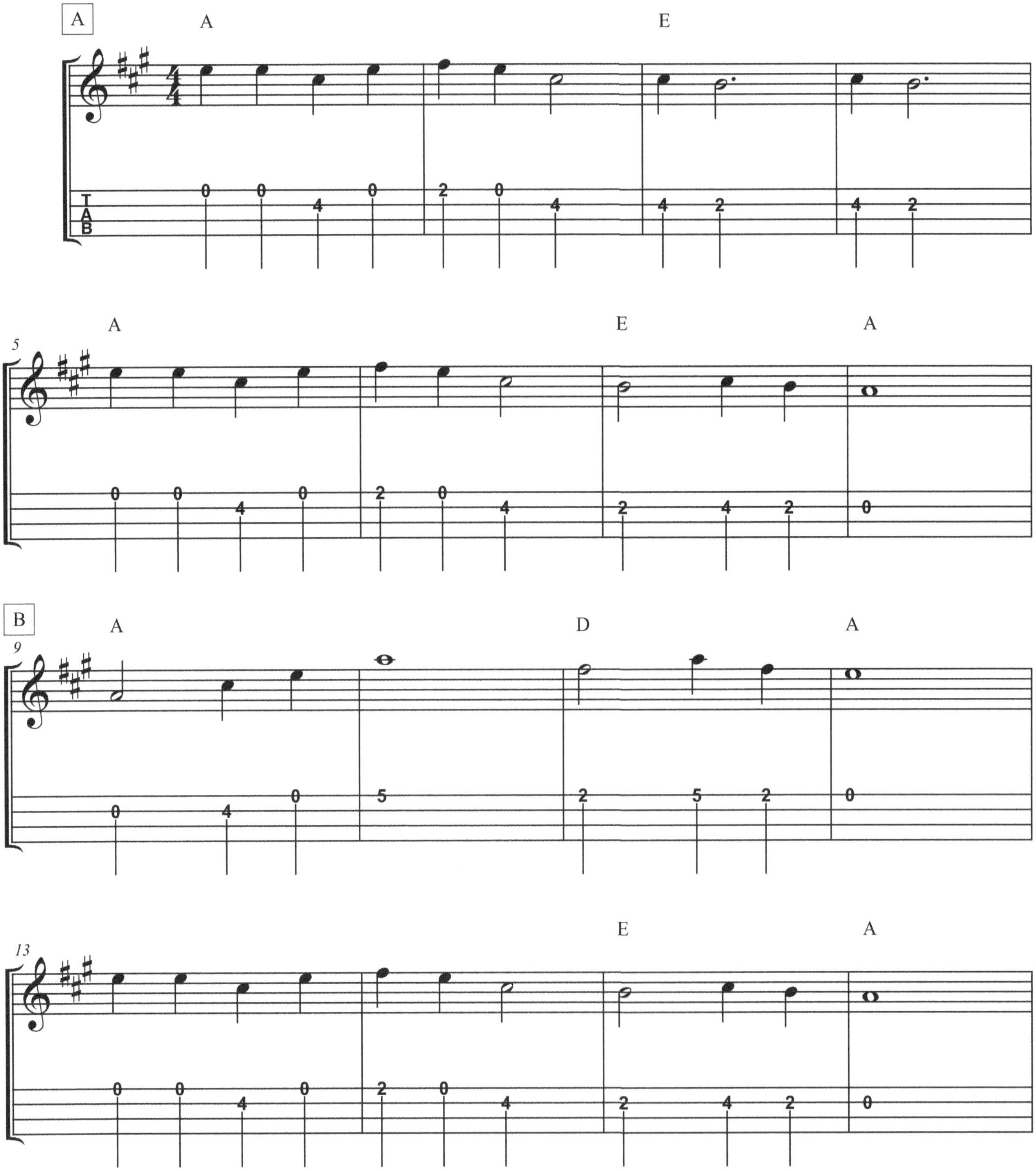

(verses sung to A part, chorus sung to B)

1. Camptown ladies sing this song
   Dooda, dooda
   Camptown racetrack's five miles long
   Oh, dooda day

2. I went down South with my hat caved in
   Dooda, dooda
   Came back North with a pocket full of tin
   Oh, dooda day

Chorus

Goin' to run all night
Goin' to run all day
I bet my money on the bob-tailed nag
Somebody bet on the bay

Cripple Creek

This American folk song comes from the Appalachian Mountains.

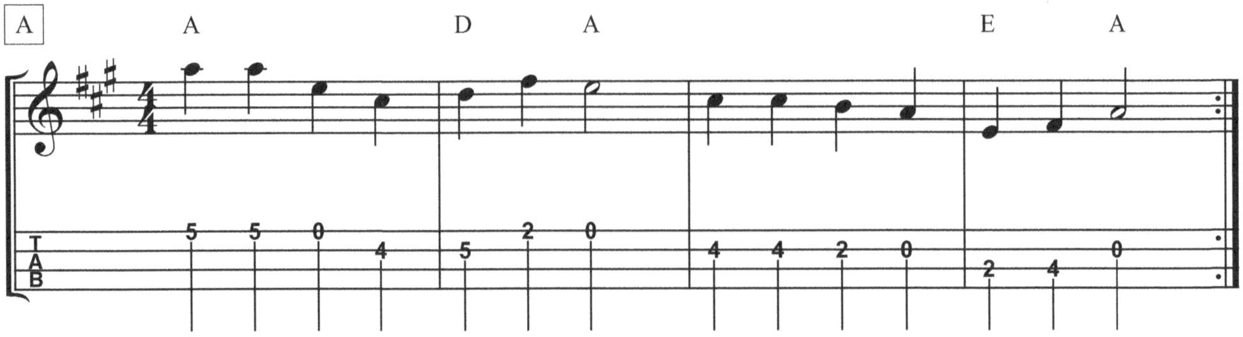

A
A D A E A

B
A E A

Rhythm Variation

A
A D A E A

B
A E A

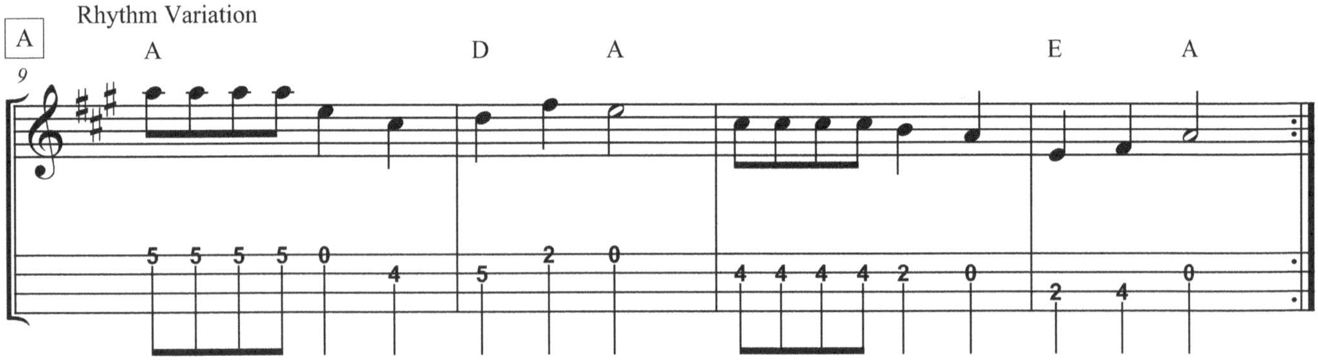

(verse sung to A part, chorus sung to B)
Goin' up Cripple Creek, goin' on the run
Goin' up Cripple Creek to have some fun
Pull my britches to my knees
Wade old Cripple Creek as I please

Chorus
Goin' up Cripple Creek goin' on the run
Goin' up Cripple Creek to have some fun
Goin' up Cripple Creek in a whirl
Goin' up Cripple Creek to see my girl

For kids and adults
Fiddle, mandolin, guitar, and more
info at www.fiddlepal.com

Buffalo Gals

A minstrel singer named Cool White wrote this song in 1844 about the beautiful gals of Buffalo, New York. Make sure you don't roll but lift your first finger off the A string and onto the E string between measures 3-4 and 11-12.

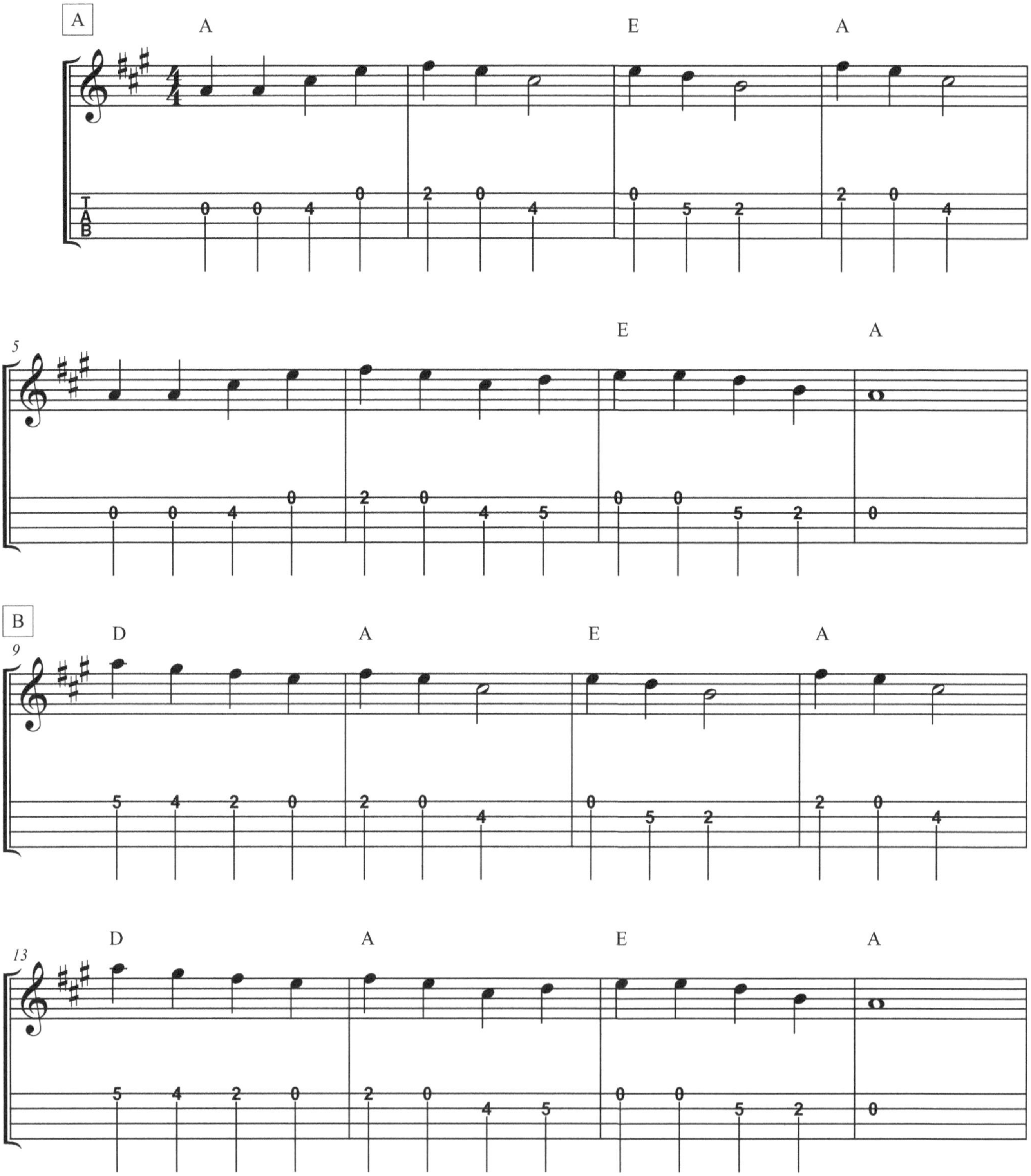

A

A E A

5

E A

B

9

D A E A

13

D A E A

(verses sung to A part, chorus sung to B)

1. As I was walking down the street
Down the street, down the street
A pretty girl I chanced to meet
And we danced by the light of the moon

Chorus
Buffalo gals won't you come out tonight
Come out tonight, come out tonight
Buffalo gals won't you come out tonight
And dance by the light of the moon

2. I asked her if she'd stop and talk
Stop and talk, stop and talk
Her feet covered up the whole sidewalk
She was fair to view

3. I asked her if she'd be my wife
Be my wife, be my wife
Then I'd be happy all my life
If she'd marry me

4. I danced with a gal with a hole in her stocking
And her heel kept a-rockin' and her knees kept a-knockin'
I danced with a gal with a hole in her stocking
And we danced by the light of the moon

Angelina Baker

Also known as Angeline the Baker, this popular folk song was also written by Stephen Foster and published in 1850. Make sure you lift not roll your third finger from the A string to the E string between measures 2-3. Note how the eighth notes in the melody relate to the pick direction. Tapping your foot on all four beats will help the picking feel more natural. Beginning at measure 17, the octave variation demonstrates how you can transpose a tune into a lower octave. Explore transposing other tunes in this book to create variety.

A

D G

T A B

5 2 0 5 0 2 0 5 5 2 0 5 2 2

5

D G D

5 2 0 5 0 2 0 5 0 2 0 5 2 0 0

B

9

D G

0 2 5 0 2 5 0 2 5 0 2 2

13

D G D

0 2 5 0 2 0 5 0 2 0 5 2 0 0

(verses and chorus sung to B part)

1. Angelina Baker she lives on the village green
   The way that I love her beats all to be seen
   Angelina Baker her age is forty-three
   I gave her candy by the peck but she won't marry me

Chorus
Angelina Baker, Angelina Baker
Angelina Baker, Angelina Baker

2. Angeline is handsome and Angeline is tall
   She broke her little ankle from dancing in the hall
   She won't do the bacon because she is too stout
   She makes cookies by the peck and throws the coffee out

3. Last time I saw her was at the county fair
   Her man he chased me half-way home and told me to stay there
   She taught me to weep and she taught me to moan
   Angeline she taught me to weep and beat on the old jawbone

Old Joe Clark

This tune was written before 1840 and is thought to be about an African-American man from Kentucky. In the third and fourth notes of measures 7, 12, and 15, leave your first finger down. It acts as a "pivot" during the string change and leaving it down makes the fingering motion efficient.

A

A E

5

A E A

B

9

A G

13

A E A

(verses sung to A part, chorus sung to B)

1. I used to live on the mountain top
Now I live in town
I'm staying at the big hotel
A-courting Betsy Brown

2. Old Joe Clark, he had a house
Sixteen stories high
And every story in that house
Was filled with chicken pie

3. Old Joe had a chicken coop
Sixteen stories high
And every chicken in that coop
Turned into chicken pie

4. Old Joe Clark, he had a mule
His name was Morgan Brown
And every tooth in that mule's head
Was sixteen inches 'round

5. I went down to Old Joe's house
He invited me to supper
I stubbed my toe on the table leg
And stuck my nose in the butter

6. Old Joe Clark's a mean old man
I'll tell you the reason why
He blew his nose in my corn bread
And called it pumpkin pie

Chorus

Fare thee well, Old Joe Clark
Fare thee well, I say
Fare thee well, Old Joe Clark
I'm a-going away

Cindy

This is an antebellum, Southern American folk song.
Make sure to use the pinky of your left handto play the 7th fret in measures 1 and 5.

(verses sung to the A part, chorus sung to B)

1. You ought to see my Cindy
   She lives way down South
   She's so sweet the honey bees
   Swarm around her mouth

Chorus
Get along home, Cindy, Cindy
Get along home
Get along home, Cindy, Cindy
I'll marry you someday

2. When first I seen my Cindy
   She was standing by the door
   Shoes and stockings in her hand
   And her little bare feet on the floor

3. Wish I was an apple
   Hangin' on a tree
   Every time my Cindy'd pass
   She'd take a bite of me

4. Cindy in the springtime
   Cindy in the fall
   If I can't have my Cindy, gal
   I'll have no gal at all

Crawdad Song

This is an early American play-party song written for children.

1. You get a line and I'll get a pole, honey
   You get a line and I'll get a pole, babe
   You get a line and I'll get a pole
   We'll go fishin' in that crawdad hole
   Honey, sugar baby, mine

2. Yonder comes a man with a sack on his back, honey
   Yonder . . . back, babe
   Yonder . . . back
   Packing all the crawdads he can pack
   Honey, sugar baby, mine

3. The man fell down and he bust his sack, honey
   The man. . . sack, babe
   The man . . . sack
   Look at them crawdads crawling back
   Honey, sugar baby, mine

4. What you gonna do when the lake runs dry. . .
   Sit on the bank and watch the crawdads die. . .

5. What you gonna do when the crawdads die, honey. . .
   Sit on the bank until I cry. . .

6. Look at that crawdad crawlin' round, honey. . .
   He's the mayor of that crawdad town. . .

7. I heard the duck say to the drake, honey. . .
   "There ain't no crawdads in this lake. . ."

Eighth Note Based Tunes

The next batch of tunes use primarily eighth notes in the melody. Pay attention to proper pick direction. Remember to check it by tapping your foot on all four beats of the measure. Your pick and foot should be moving in the same direction.

Bonaparte's Retreat

This is a very old fiddle tune from the Appalachian Mountains.

Red Haired Boy

This Irish tune is also known as "The Little Beggar Man."
Pay attention to your pick direction and make sure to follow the arrows in some of the trickier sections.

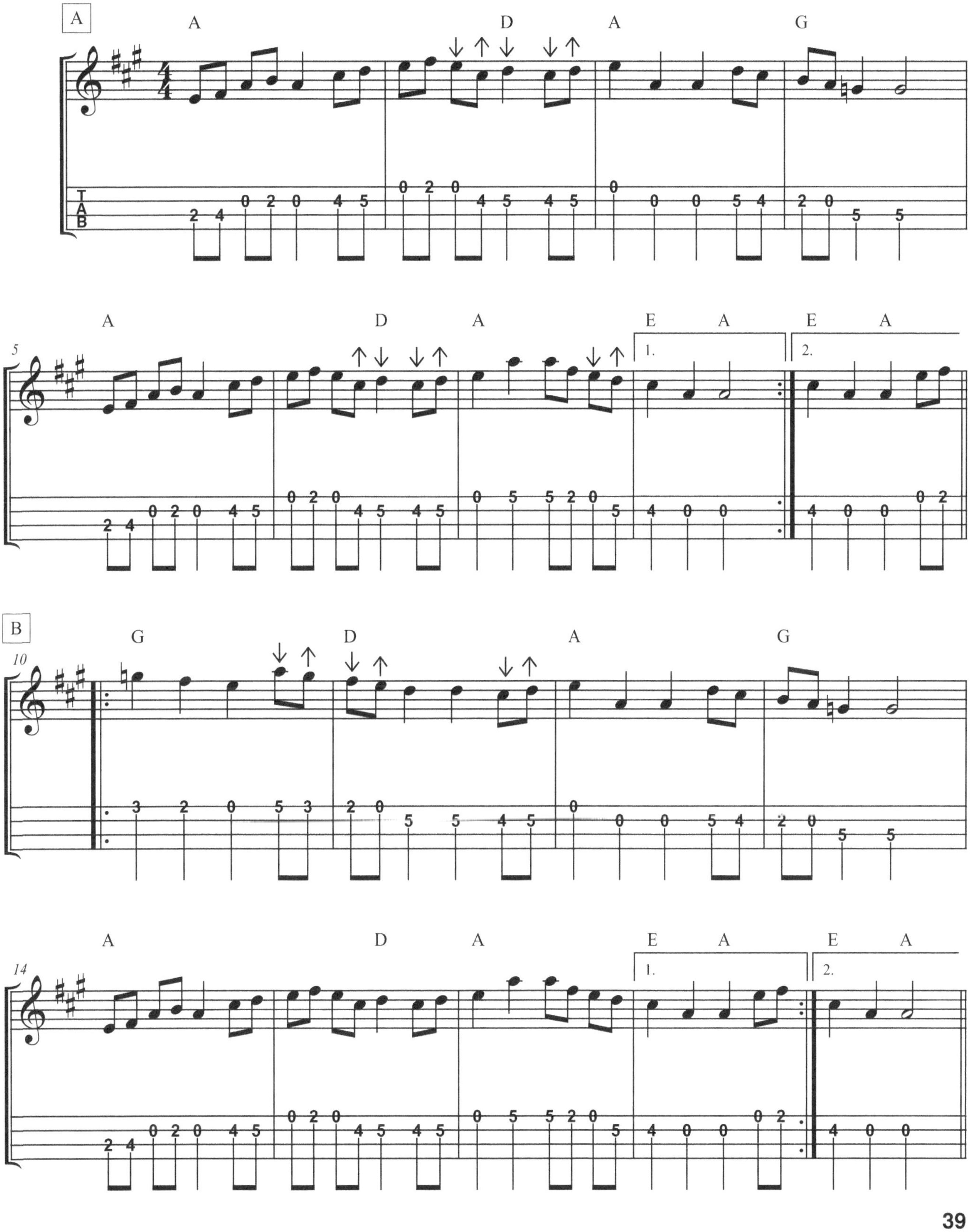

Country Waltz

This old-time American tune is played throughout the United States. Note the triplet at the beginning of measure 15. Pay close attention to the pick direction arrows.

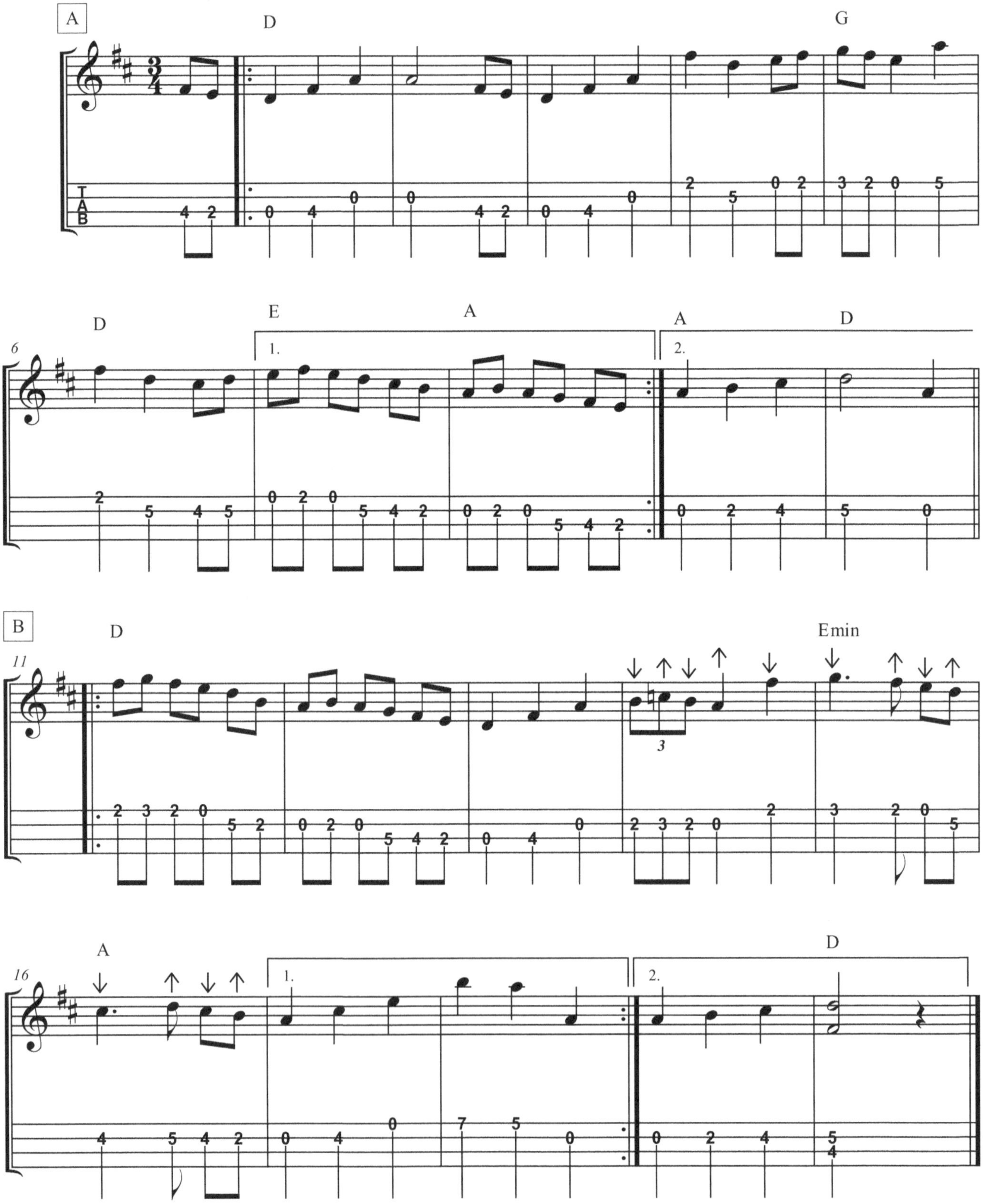

Girl I Left Behind Me

The melody can be traced to the 1750s in England and is still often played by the British Navy.

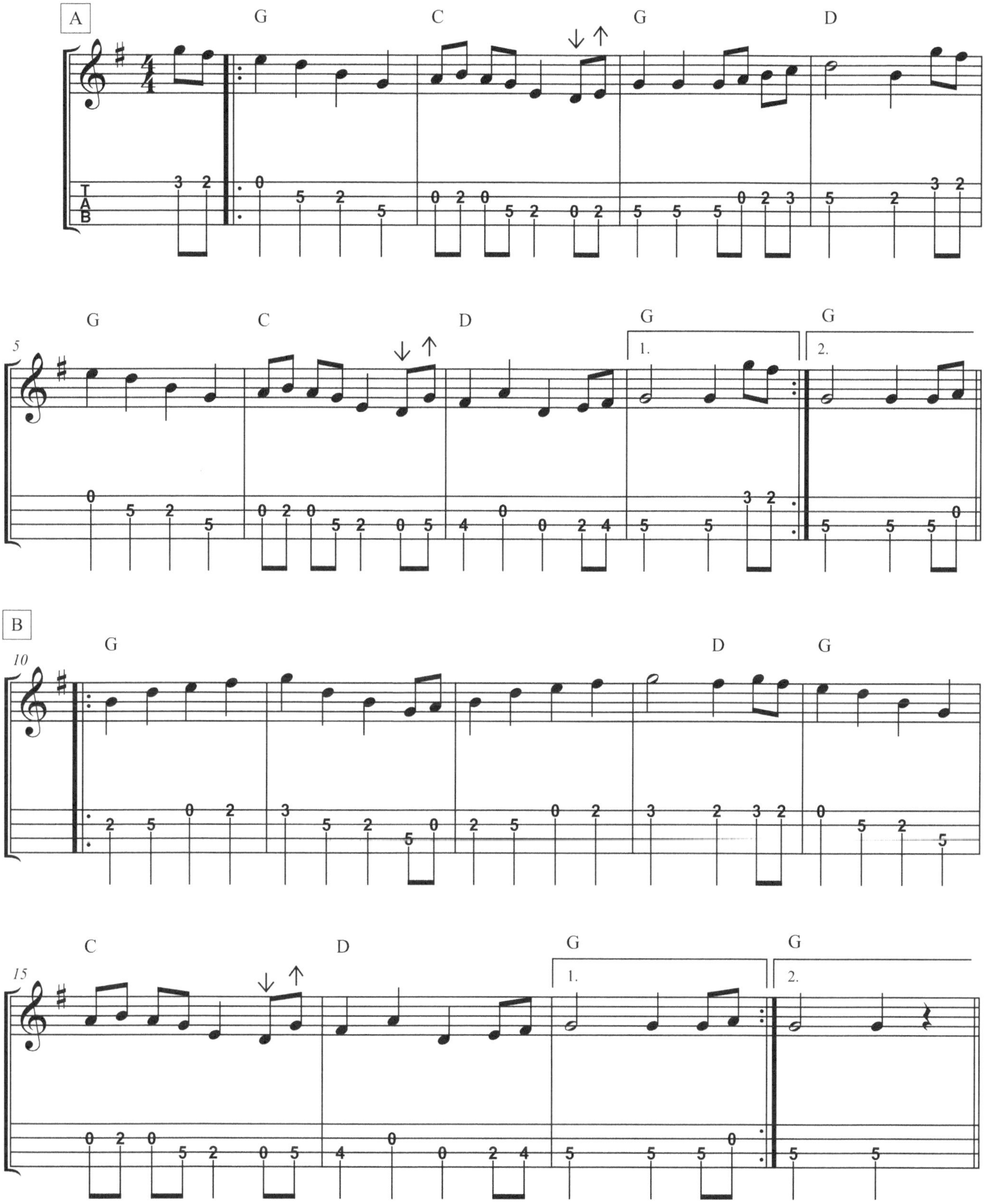

Tremolo

Tremolo is the technique of rapidly playing a single note. A single, plucked note from a mandolin has very short sustain. Tremolo is a way to give notes longer sustain and greater expression. It sounds especially good on slow tunes such as the following next three: *Down in the Valley*, *Amazing Grace*, and *Red River Valley*.

Counterintuitive as it may seem, tremolo doesn't come from *trying* to pick faster, but rather from relaxing your wrist and allowing your hand to jiggle – almost like one of those rubber hands from the joke shop! Some players have remarked that only when they quit *trying* so hard, did their tremolo start to sound natural. Some mandolin players describe the feeling in their right hand and wrist as "brave, but loose."

There are no rules for how fast the tremolo is to be played. It can vary from slow (a little faster than eighth notes), to a blur of lighting fast notes. It's good to master a variety of speeds in your playing so you can choose which speed works best. Tremolo is indicated by three lines across the note stem.

When you play the tremolo, don't worry about the number of pick strokes you play, but pay attention to how the duration of the note relates to the underlying rhythm of the song. End the tremolo with a down stroke. This will help you to smoothly transition out of the tremolo and ensure that your pick is moving in the correct direction as you resume standard picking.

The next three songs sound great with tremolo. Listen to the CD to copy the speed, duration and phrasing of the tremolo. *Remember to keep your wrist loose and end on a down stroke.*

Down in the Valley

An early American folk ballad in waltz time.

Down in the valley, valley so low
Hang your head over, hear the wind blow
Hear the wind blow, dear, hear the wind blow
Hang your head over, hear the wind blow

Roses love sunshine, violets love dew
Angels in Heaven know I love you
Know I love you, dear, know I love you
Angels in Heaven know I love you

Build me a castle, forty feet high
So I can see her as she rides by
As she rides by, dear, as she rides by
So I can see her as she rides by

If you don't love me, love whom you please
Throw your arms round me, give my heart ease
Give my heart ease, dear, give my heart ease
Throw your arms round me, give my heart ease

Write me a letter, send it by mail
Send it in care of the Birmingham jail
Birmingham jail, dear, Birmingham jail
Send it in care of the Birmingham jail

Amazing Grace

English poet and clergyman John Newton wrote this hymn which has become one of the most recognizable songs in the English-speaking world.

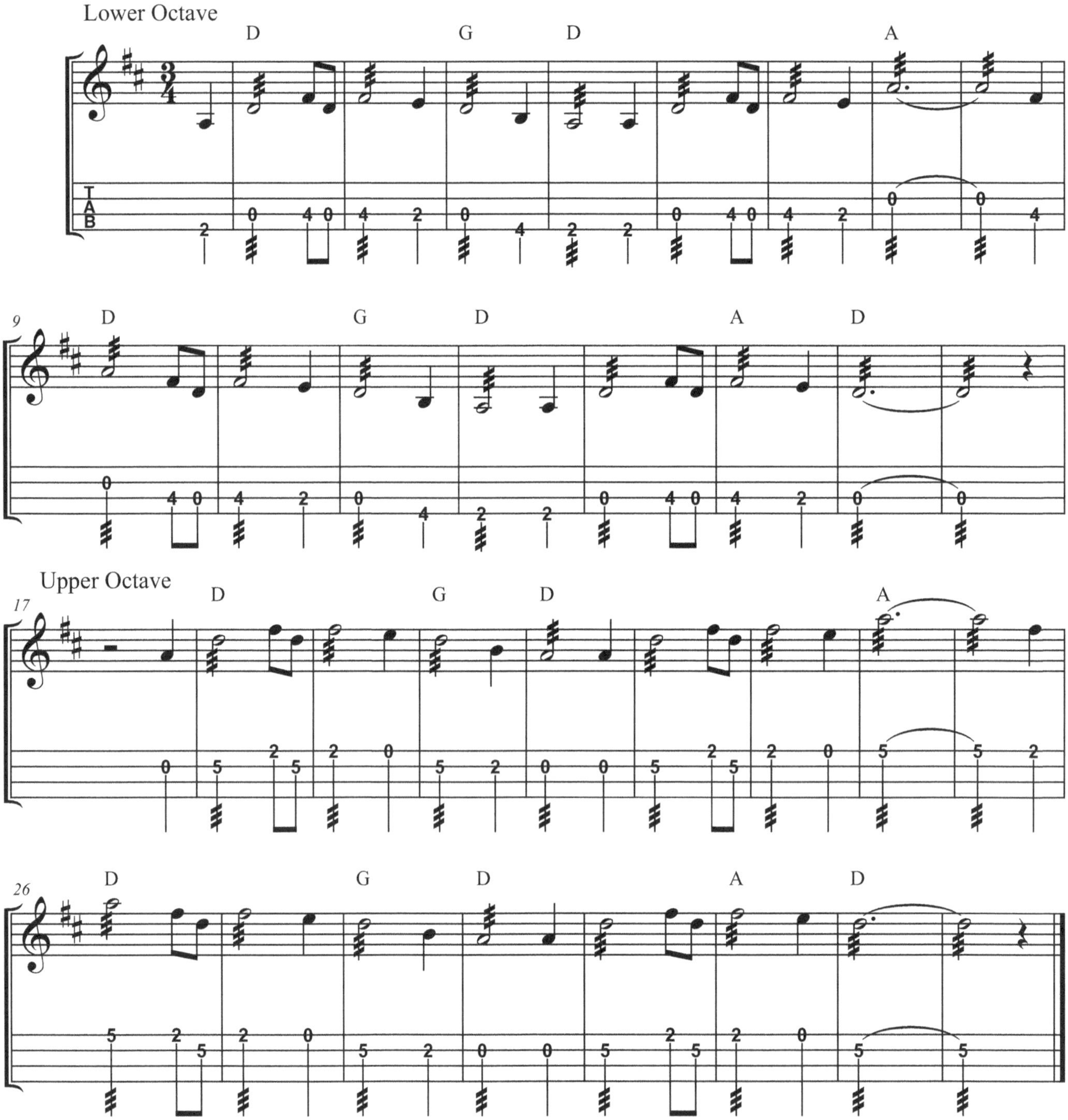

Lower Octave

D G D A D G D A D

Upper Octave

D G D A D G D A D

Amazing Grace, how sweet the sound
That saved a wretch like me
I once was lost but now am found
Was blind, but now, I see

T'was grace that taught my heart to fear
And grace my fears relieved
How precious did that grace appear
The hour I first believed

Through many dangers, toils and snares
We have already come
T'was grace that brought us safe thus far
And grace will lead us home

Red River Valley

This is a popular early American cowboy folk song.

1. From this valley they say you are going
   We will miss your bright eyes and sweet smile
   For they say you are taking the sunshine
   That has brightened our pathways awhile

Chorus
Come and sit by my side, if you love me
Do not hasten to bid me adieu
Just remember the Red River Valley
And the cowboy who loved you so true

2. I've been thinking a long time, my darling
   Of the sweet words you never would say
   Now, alas, must my fond hopes all vanish?
   For they say you are going away

3. Do you think of the valley you're leaving?
   O how lonely and how dreary it will be
   And do you think of the kind hearts you're breaking?
   And the pain you are causing to me?

4. They will bury me where you have wandered
   Near the hills where the daffodils grow
   When you're gone from the Red River Valley
   For I can't live without you I know

Shady Grove

This 18th century folk song is popular in Celtic and bluegrass circles. Musicologists have documented over 100 verses to this song!

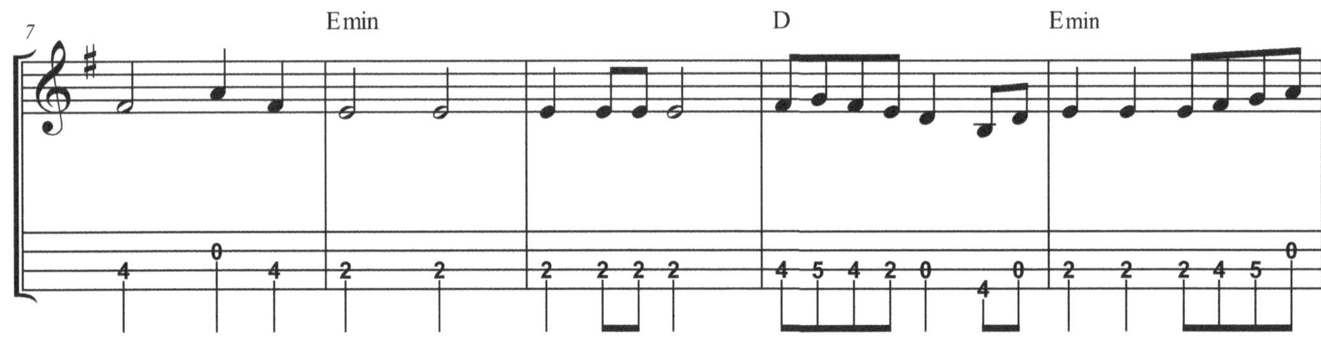

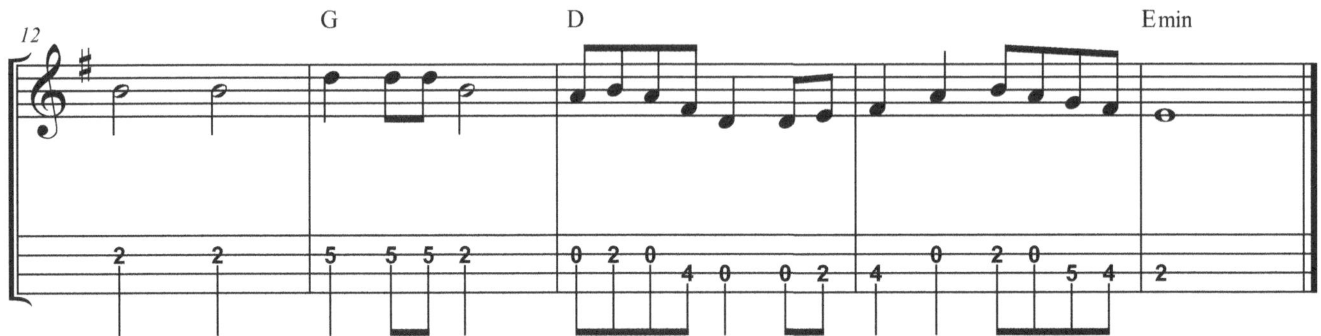

1. Cheeks as red a a blooming rose
   And eyes the prettiest brown
   She's the darling of my heart
   Stay 'til the sun goes down

Chorus
   Shady Grove, my little love
   Shady Grove I say
   Shady Grove, my little love
   I'm bound to go away

2. The last time I saw Shady Grove
   She was standing in the door
   Her shoes and stockings in her hand
   And her little bare feet on the floor

3. I wish I had a big fine horse
   And corn to feed him on
   And a pretty little girl to stay at home
   And feed him when I'm gone

4. When I was a little boy
   I wanted a Barlow knife
   And now I want little Shady Grove
   To say she'll be my wife

Sugar Hill

Thought to be an old minstrel tune, this one dates back to the early 1800s. "Sugar Hill" is said to signify the wild part of town.

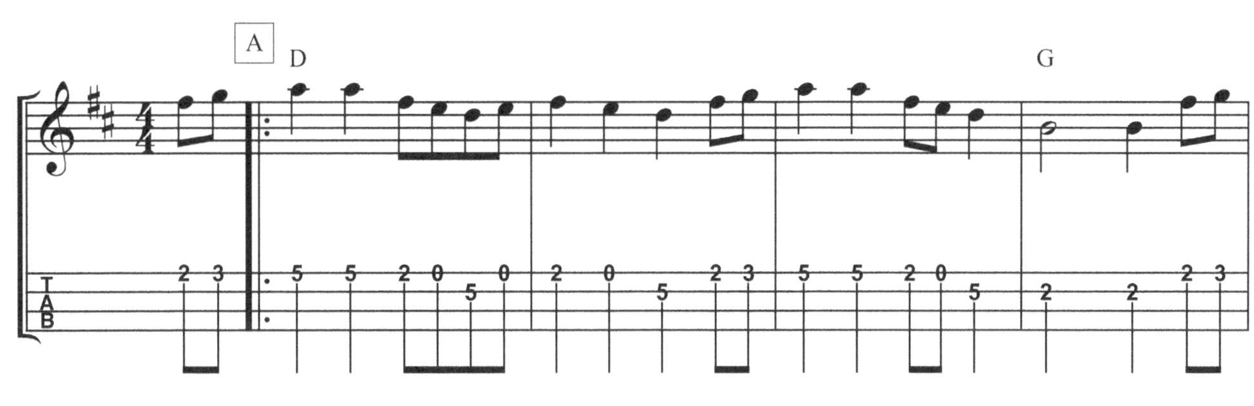

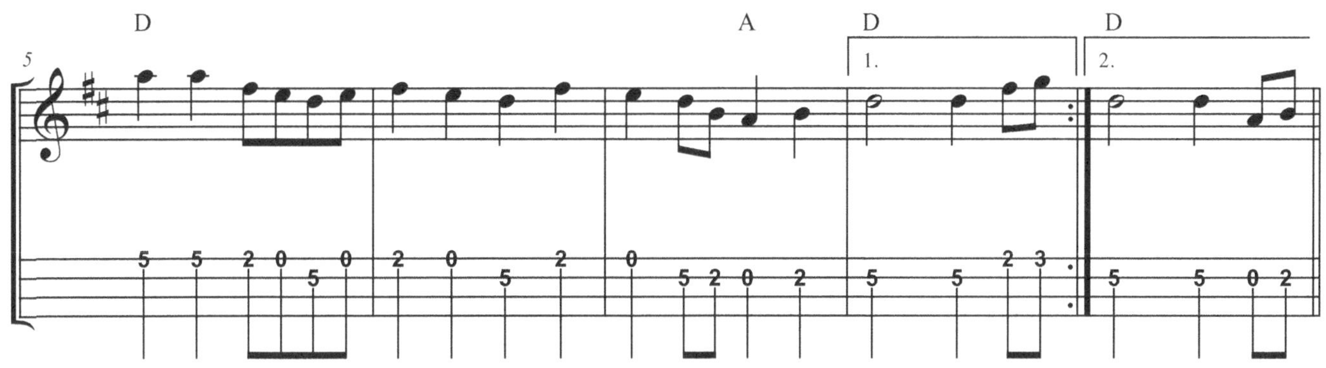

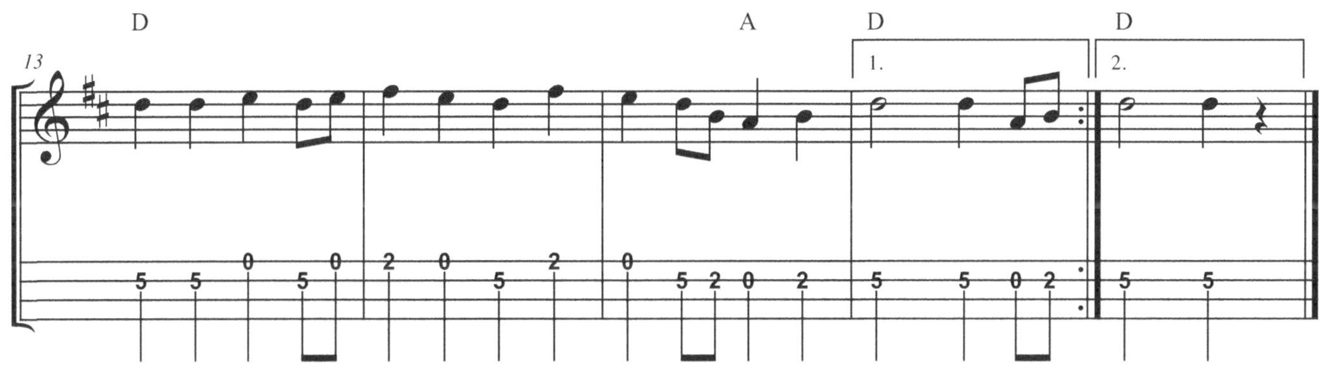

Cluck Old Hen

This is a popular Appalachian fiddle and banjo tune. It is played either as an instrumental or with lyrics. The earliest recording is attributed to Fiddlin' John Carson, in 1923.

1. My old hen she's a good old hen
   She lays eggs for the railroad men
   Sometimes one, sometimes two
   Sometimes enough for the whole damn crew

Chorus
Cluck old hen cluck and sing
You ain't laid an egg since late last spring
Cluck old hen cluck and squall
Ain't laid an egg since late last fall

2. Had an ol' hen, had a wooden leg
   Best ol' hen that ever laid an egg
   Laid more eggs than any hen around the farm
   'nother nip o' whiskey won't do me any harm

Arran Boat Song

This type of slow, mournful Irish tune is called an "air."
This tune is named after the islands off the west coast of Ireland. To break up the predictability of playing tremolo on every first beat, explore mixing in singly plucked notes as in measures 3, 4, 11, 12, 19 and 20.

A

Emin D Emin

7 D A

B

Emin G D

13 Emin G A Emin

19 G D Emin D A

Over the Waterfall

This fiddle tune has been played on both sides of the Atlantic since the early 19th century.

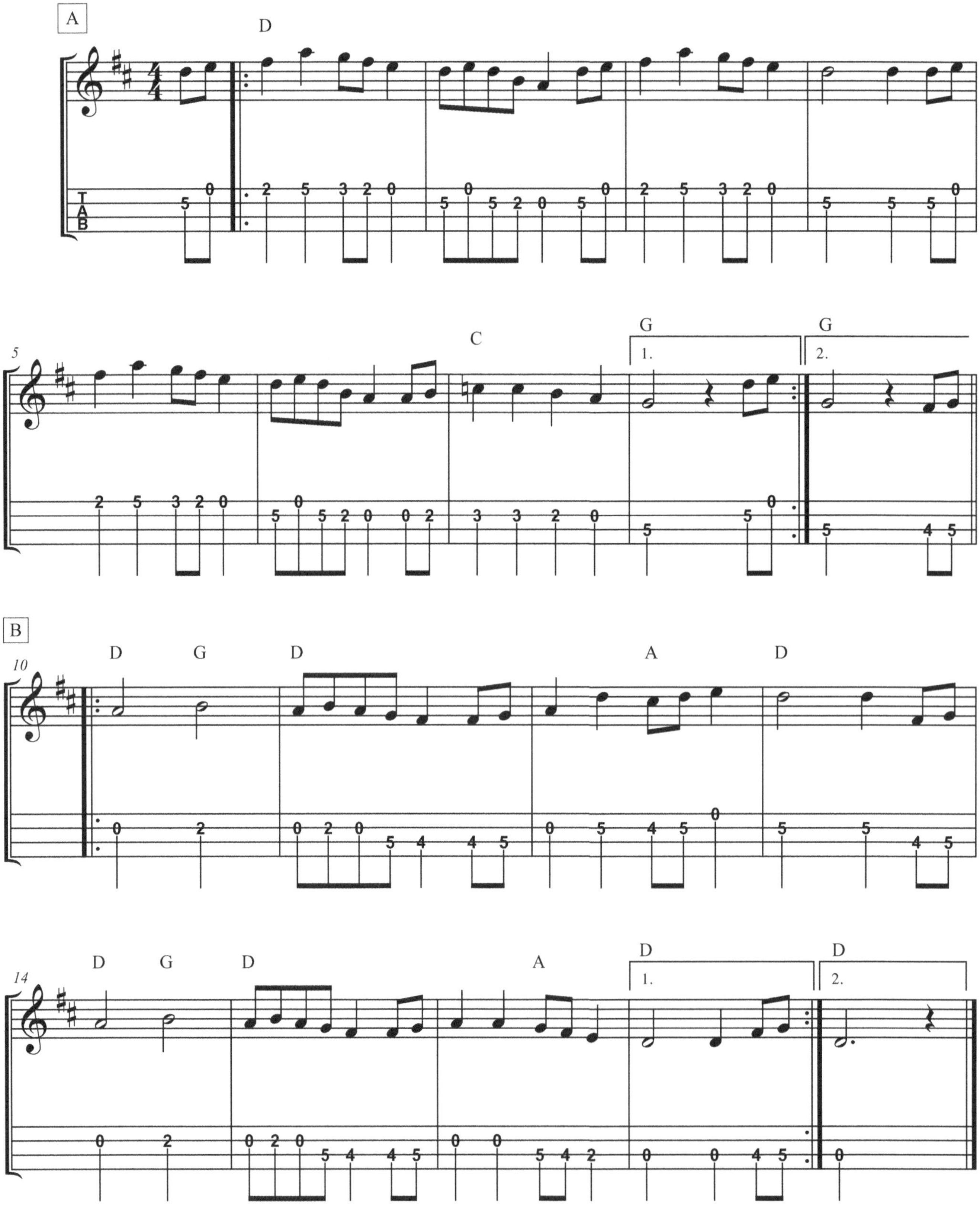

For the authors' performing and teaching schedule, books and recordings visit:

www.fiddlepal.com

www.benwinship.com

Si Beag Si Mor

The first tune ever composed by the famed Irish harpist Turlough 'O Carolan in the 1600s. Note on the accompanying CD how we varied up the tremolo and the single notes.

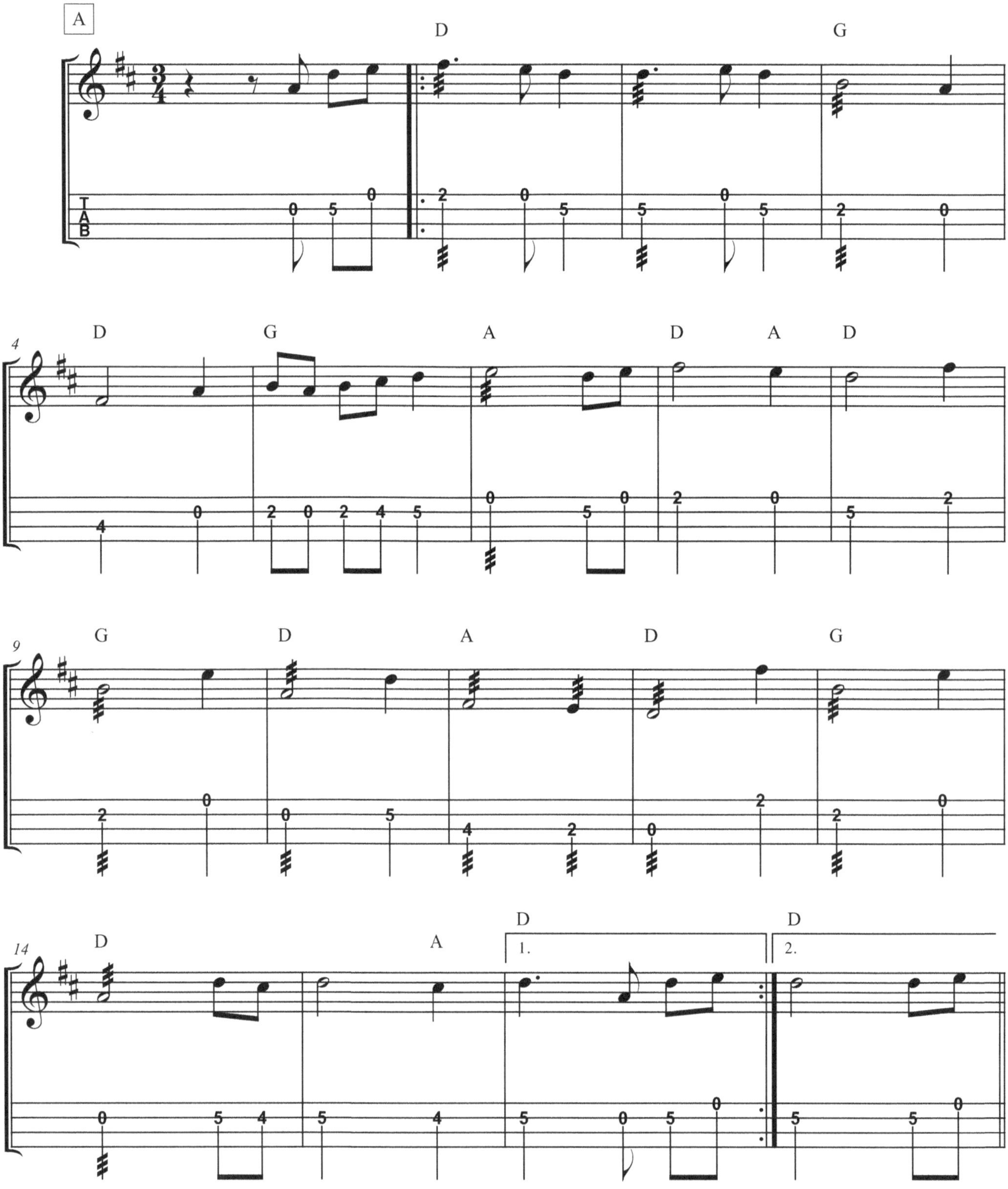

A

B
D
G
D
A
D
Bmin
A
D
A
D
G
D
G
A
D
A
D
D
1.
2.

Sandy Boys

This popular old-time fiddle tune comes from the Appalachian Mountains.

Southwind

This tune is an Irish waltz. To break up the predictability of playing tremolo on every first beat, explore mixing in singly–plucked notes.

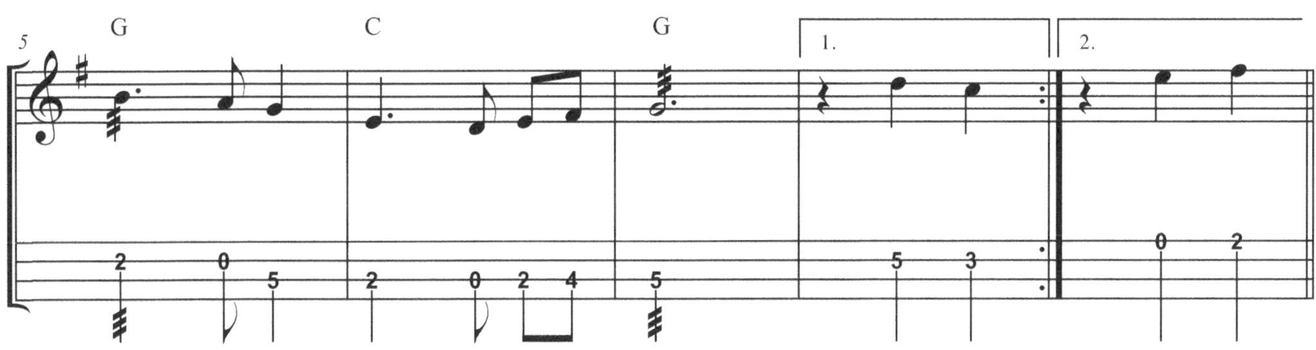

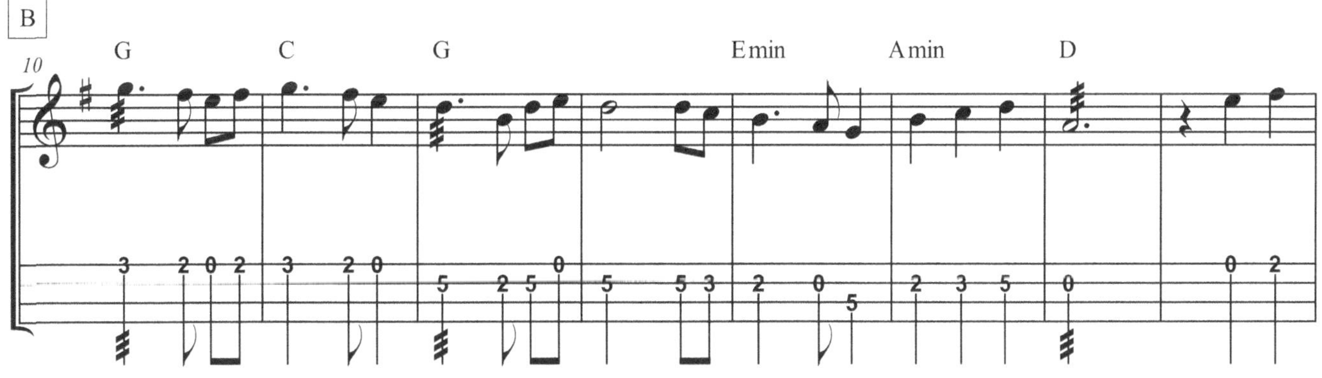

Red Wing

The melody to this song about an American-Indian girl who is saddened by the loss of her sweetheart in battle is now more commonly played as an instrumental. It was written by Thurland Cattaway and Kerry Mills in 1907.

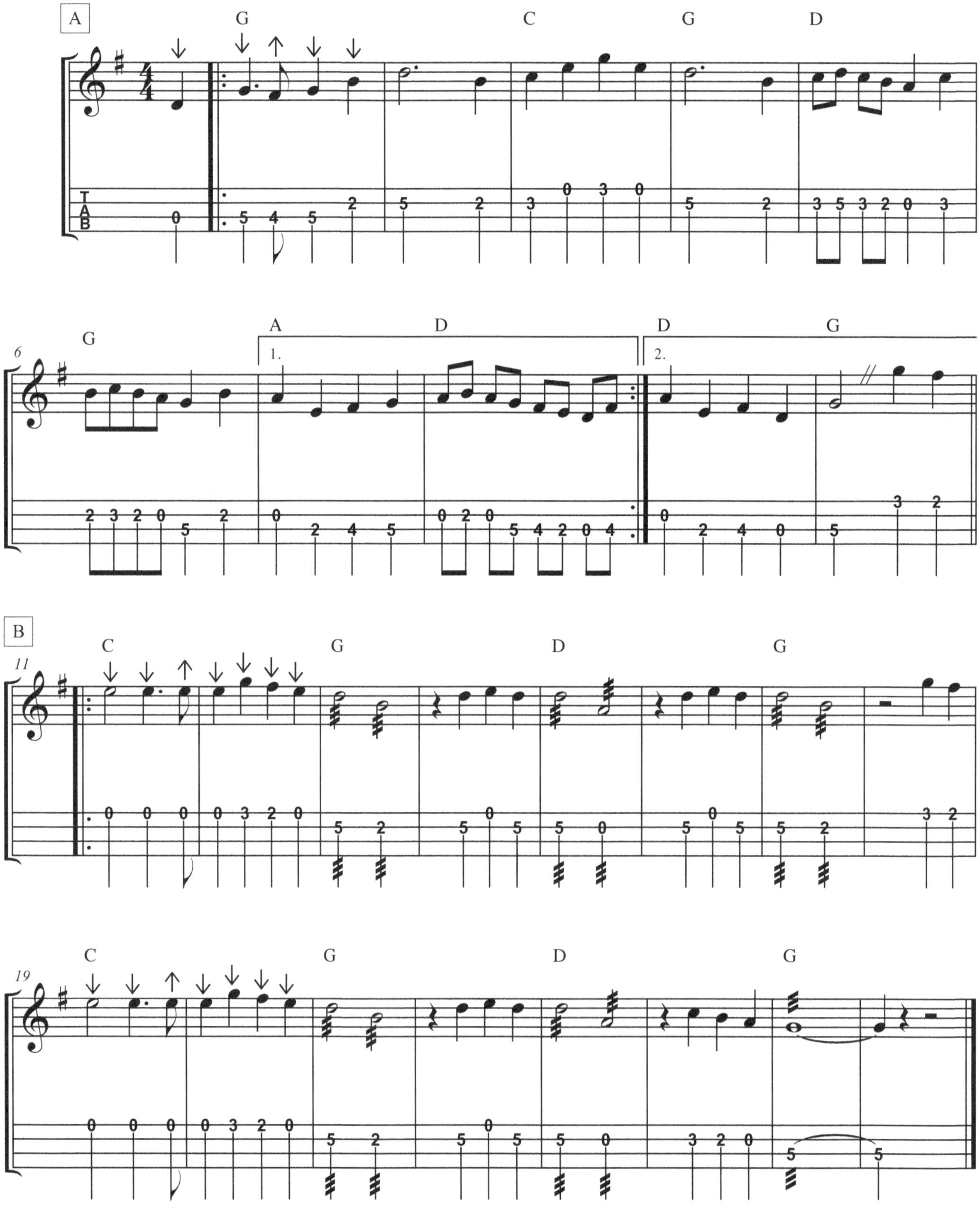

Cairo

This tune was probably written about the town of Cairo (pronounced "kay-roe"), in the southern tip of Illinois, near the borders of Kentucky and Missouri.

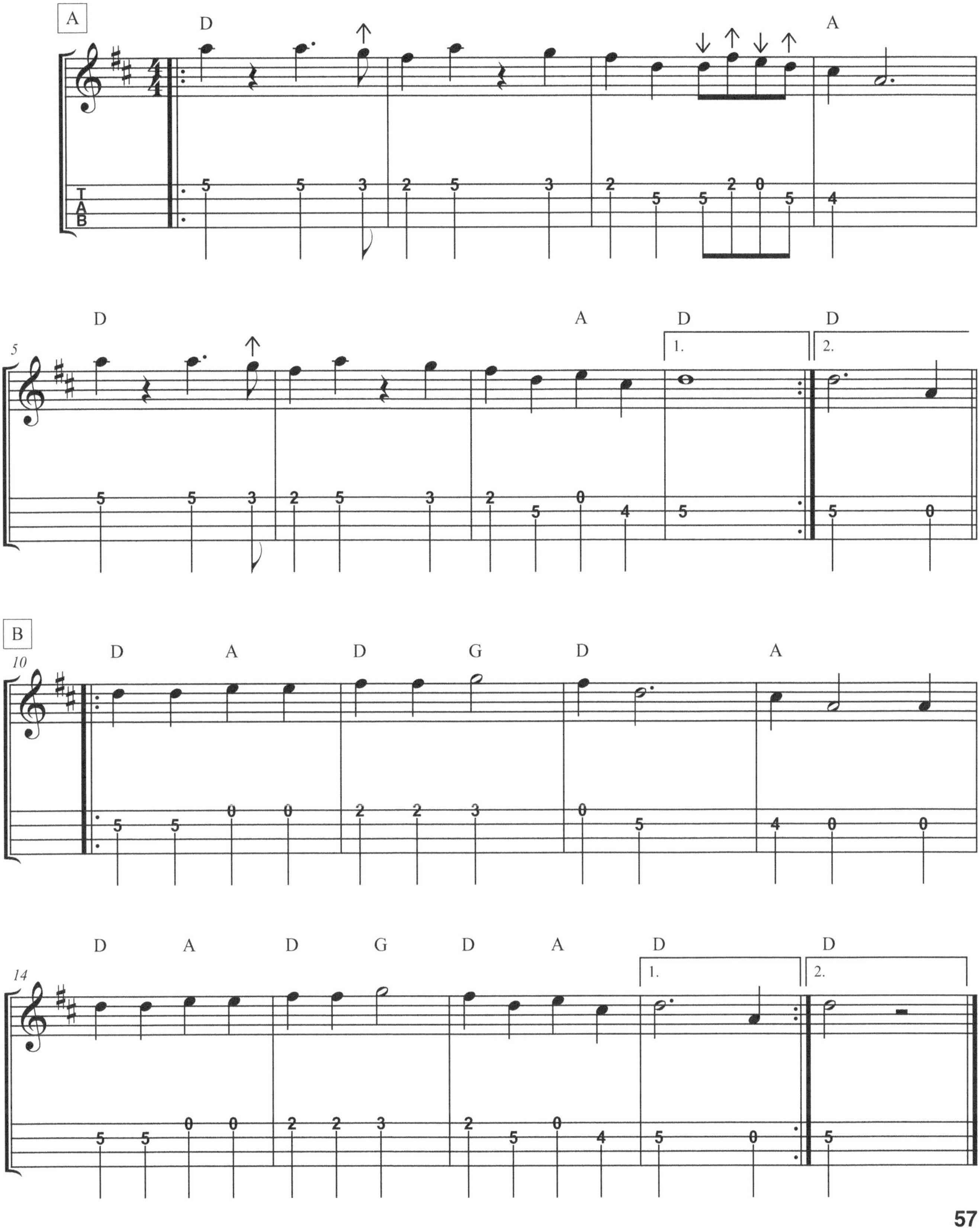

Miss McLeod's Reel

This traditional tune is popular with both Celtic fiddlers in the British Isles and old-time players in the US. It has the same melody as the song, "Did You Ever See the Devil, Uncle Jo?"

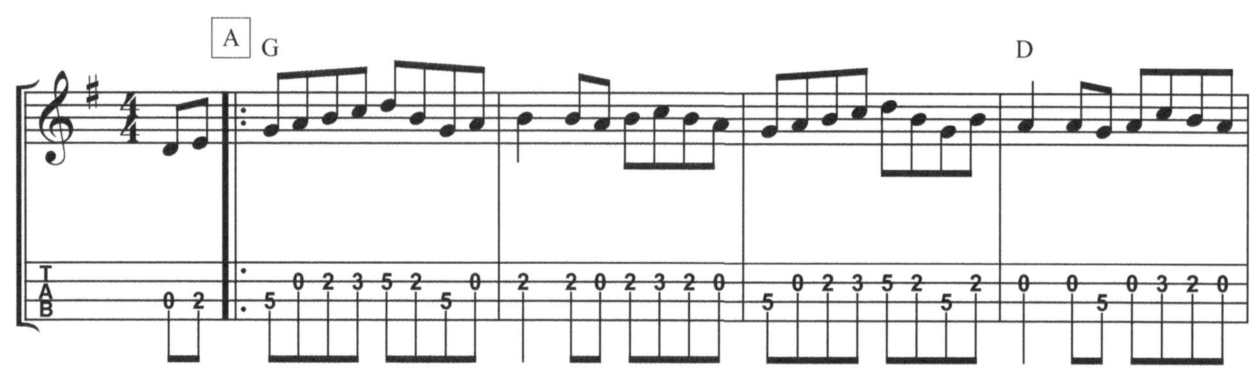

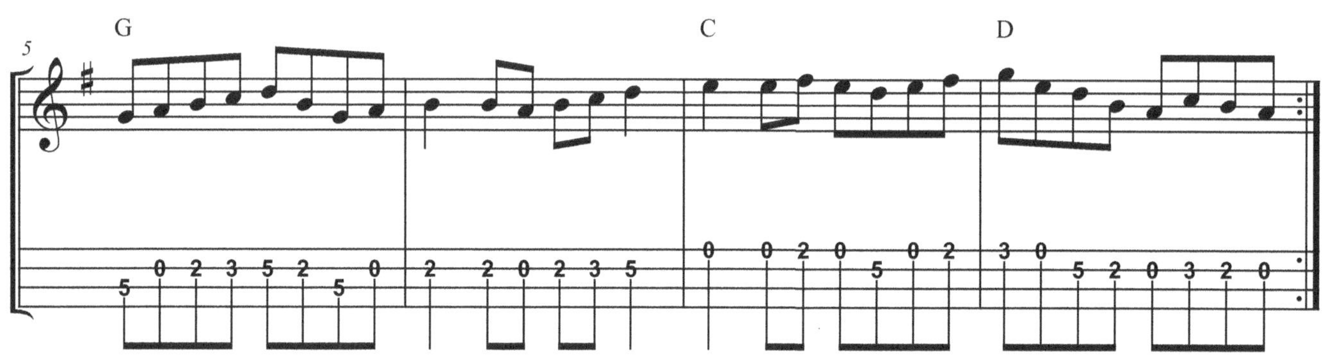

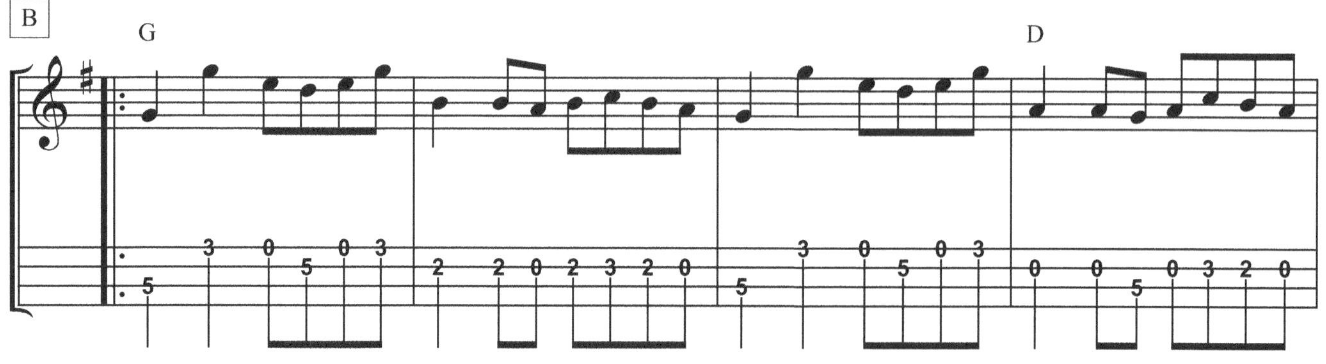

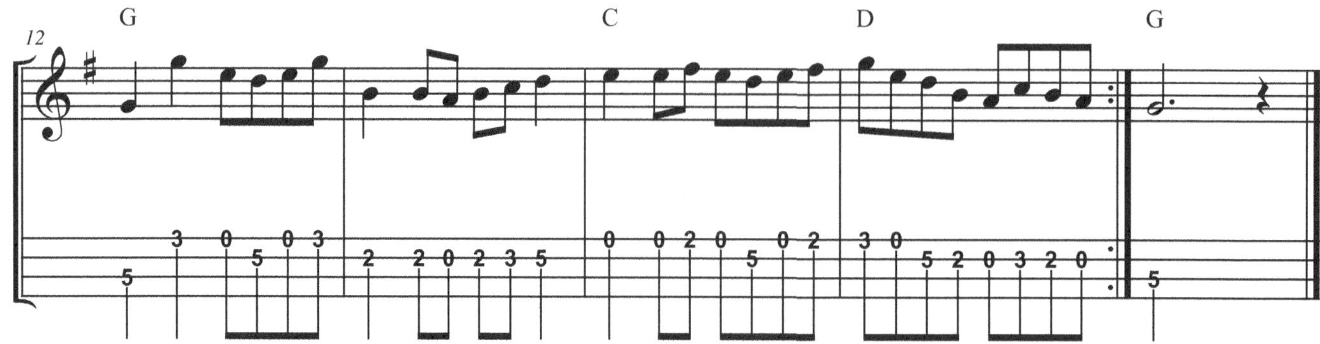

Turkey in the Straw

This is a midwestern tune was first played in the 1830s. Over the years, endless verses have been written to its melody. There is some tricky picking in the B section – pay close attention to the arrows.

G D

5 G D G D G

1. 2.

B

10 G C

14 G D G D G

Stinky's Blues

This tune follows the 12-bar blues format. The variations of this tune are common in many blues tunes. Listen to the accompanying CD to get the feel for this one.

A

A

5 D A E

10 A Go On E Last Time A Fine

Fine

B

14 A

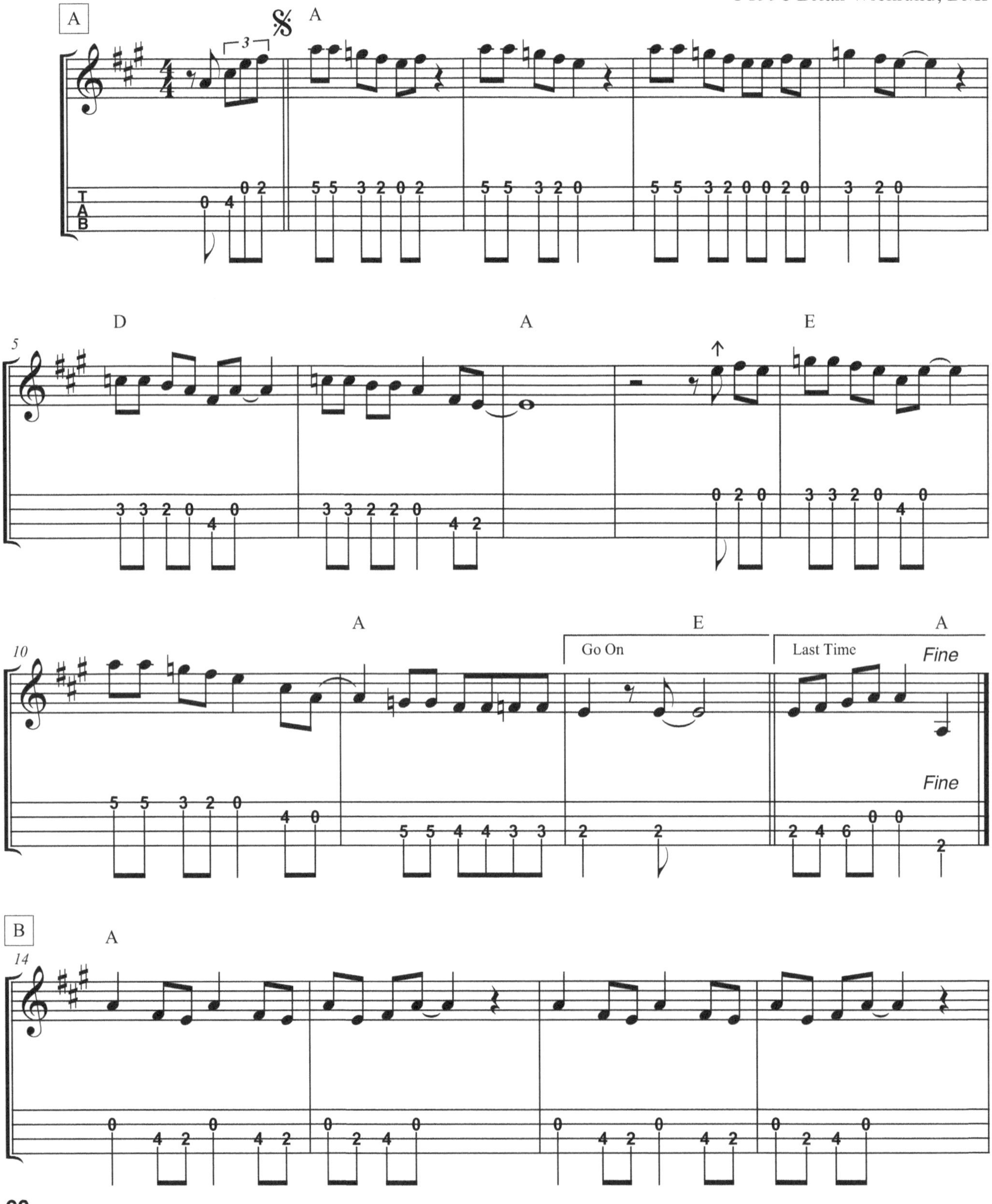

18
D
A
22
E
A
E
C
26
A
30
D
A
34
E
A
D.S. al Fine
E

Jamming

Playing in a good jam session is the reward for all of your diligent practicing. You get to meet people like yourself who love to play music, play the tunes you've practiced with other instruments, and get ideas for variations and new tunes.

To avoid etiquette faux pas, it's important to know what type of jam you are in. All jam sessions can be grouped into three types: Playing Parts, Unison, and Trading Solos Jams.

Playing Parts Jams

These jams are structured around people playing parts that are predetermined by a composer. Parts are either read or are memorized; such as in a classical ensemble. In the early 20th century, mandolin orchestras were common across the US. These days most major cities have one or more mandolin orchestras.

Unison Jams

In these jams all lead instruments play the melody together. These types of sessions are usually based on fiddle tunes. Irish, old-time Appalachian, Swedish, Scottish, and Canadian are examples of styles where mandolins would usually join the fiddles in playing the melody. No one takes solos or improvises in this style of jam. Instead, the fun comes from the power and rhythm of a group playing the same melody together. If you don't know the melody, you can play the chords instead.

Trading Solos Jams

In these jams musicians each take turns playing a solo in the tune. Music styles such as bluegrass, jazz, swing, blues, and rock use this format. When not playing a solo, the mandolin plays chords. These jams are fun because everyone has an opportunity to "show their stuff." You also get a chance to play variations or improvise.

Before entering a jam session, it's important to understand which of the three formats the jam session will follow. Inadvertent blunders such as a bluegrasser improvising at a unison-type Appalachian jam, or an Irish player playing the melody over someone else's solo in a bluegrass jam are avoided by understanding which type of jam you've joined.

The tunes in the recording that accompanies this book have all been recorded in the solo style; even the tunes that are traditionally played in unison. It is important to know the chords to each of the tunes you learn so you can jam in the unison style or the solo style. Both kinds of jams are challenging and fun.

CHORDS

Learn the chords to all of the tunes you play. This will allow you to jam with other musicians and begin to see the relationship between a chord and the melody it harmonizes.

There are many levels of understanding chords and backup playing. In *American Mandolin Method, Volume 2* we will discuss basic music theory and many more chord positions than we present in this book. However, for now we will keep it simple by presenting one **open chord** and one **chop chord** formation for each of the chords used in the book.

Teach yourself to use open chords and chop chords by following this guide:

1. Muscle memorize each chord so that you can play them cleanly (without muffled or buzzing strings).
2. Select three chords, practice switching between them with a metronome so that you can make the chord changes without pausing (start with A, D and E chords). Experiment with eight beats per chord. Then practice four beats per chord, then two beats. (Eventually you should practice switching between every possible combination of chords).
3. Learn to play the example tunes in this section.
4. Play along with the recording. Practice smoothly transitioning within a tune from playing the chords–to playing the melody–to playing the chords.
5. Finally, get together with other musicians and jam!

Open Chords and Rhythm

The easiest chords to learn are open chords. They are called open because they include some unfretted, or "open" strings. They are rich and full sounding. Below are open chord formations for each chord used in this book:

Open Chords

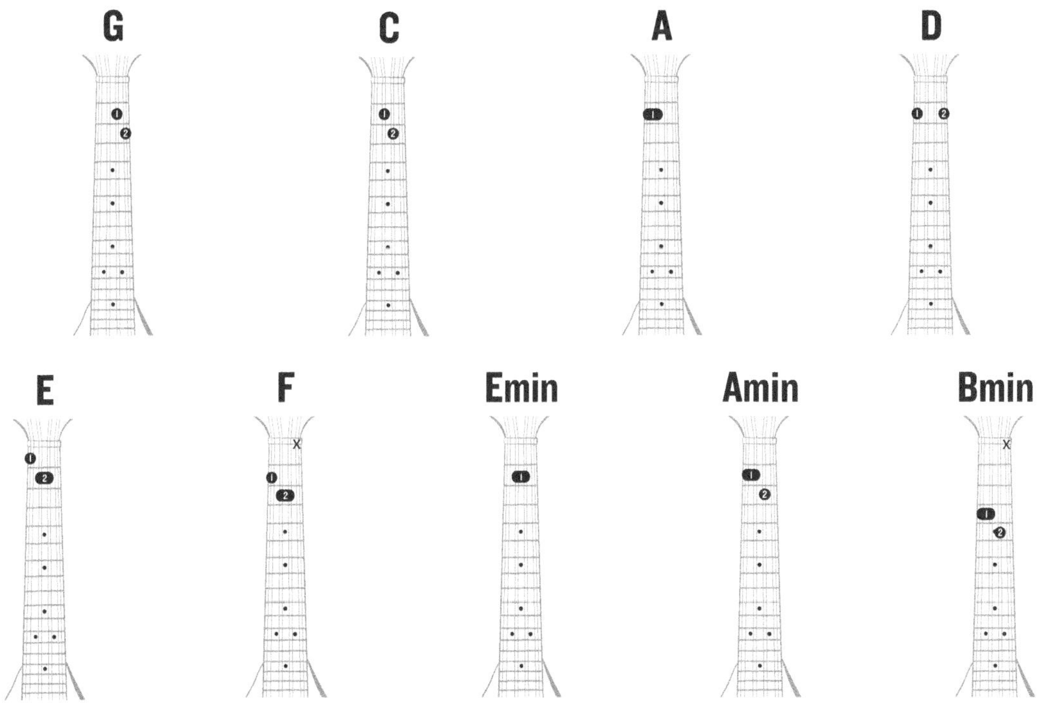

G C A D

E F Emin Amin Bmin

x = don't play that string

Camptown Races Chords

Set your metronome to 80 BPM and sing the melody. Strum across all 8 strings with simple down strokes on the 1st and 3rd beats of each measure. Strive to change chords in time with the rhythm.

Now sing and strum down strokes on all four beats of the measure.

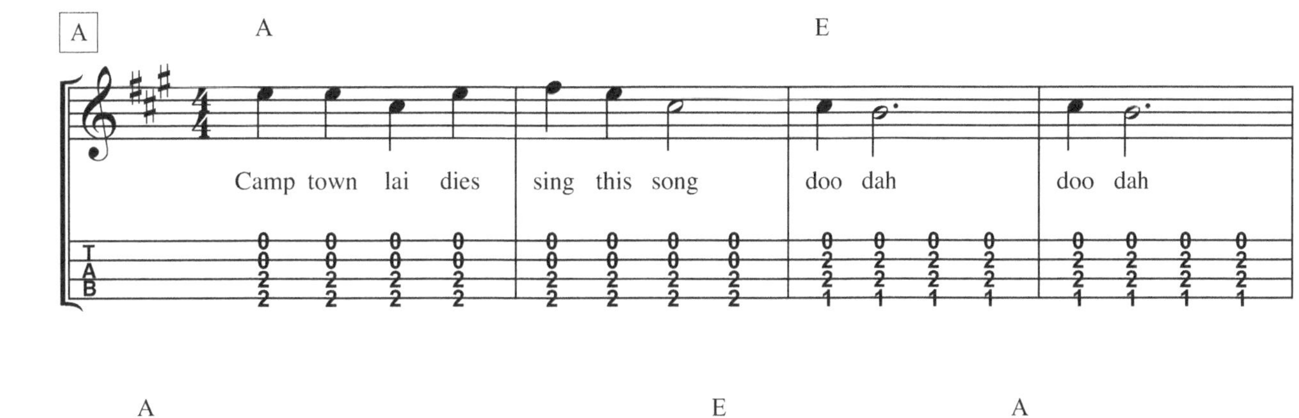

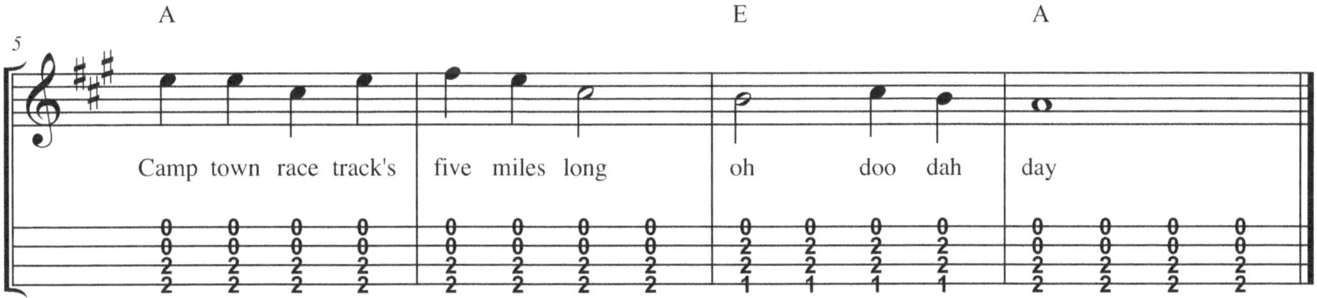

Now experiment with this rhythm. It's "one, two *and* three, four."

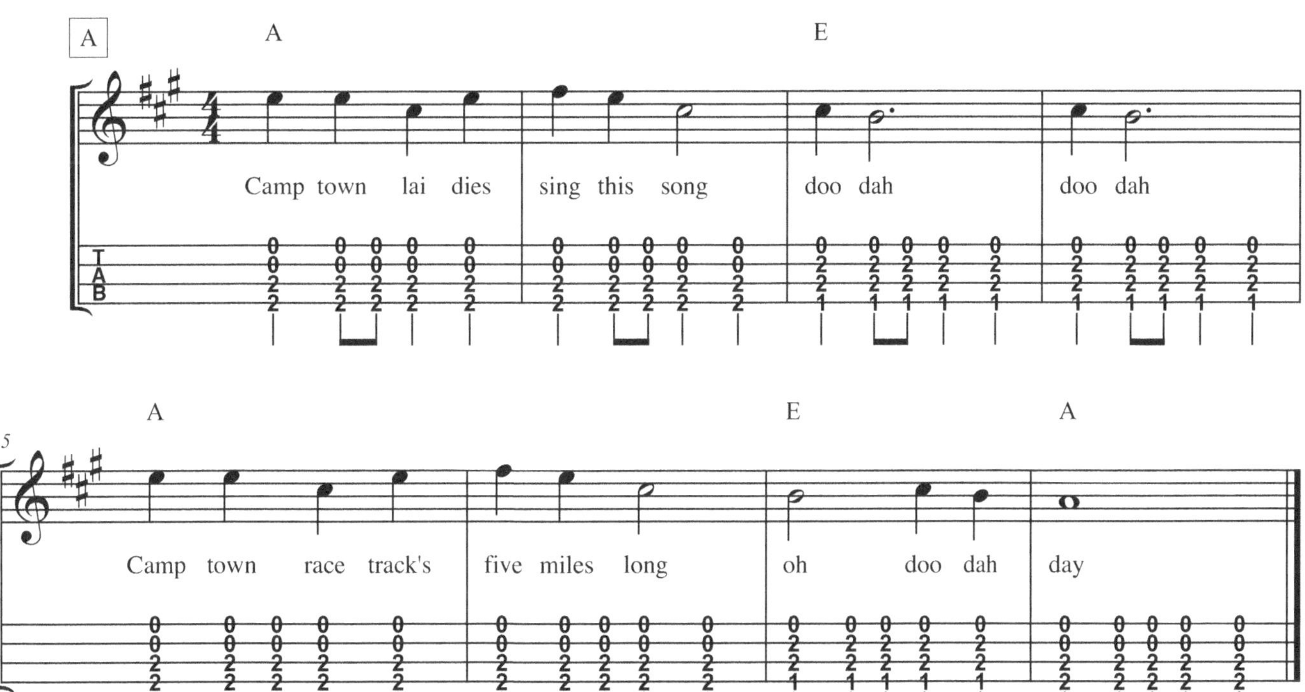

Experiment with this rhythm that goes "one, two, three *and* four *and*."

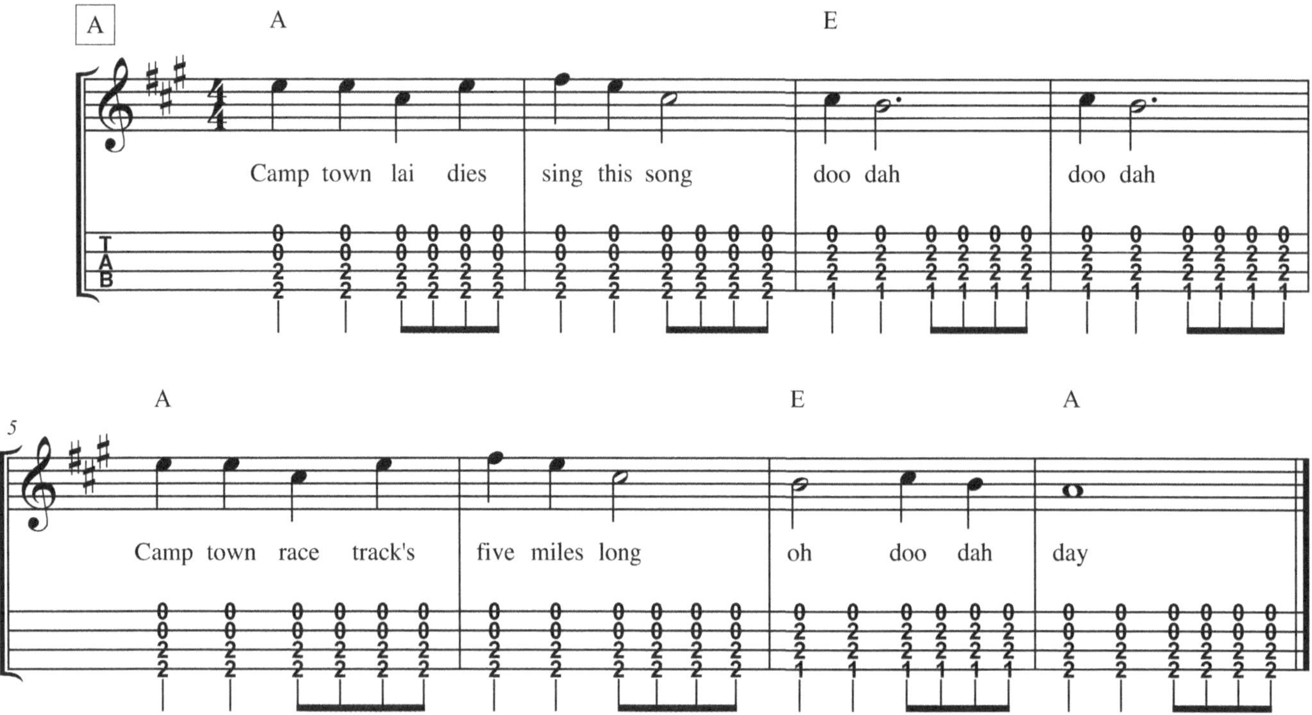

This one goes "one *and* two *and* three, four."

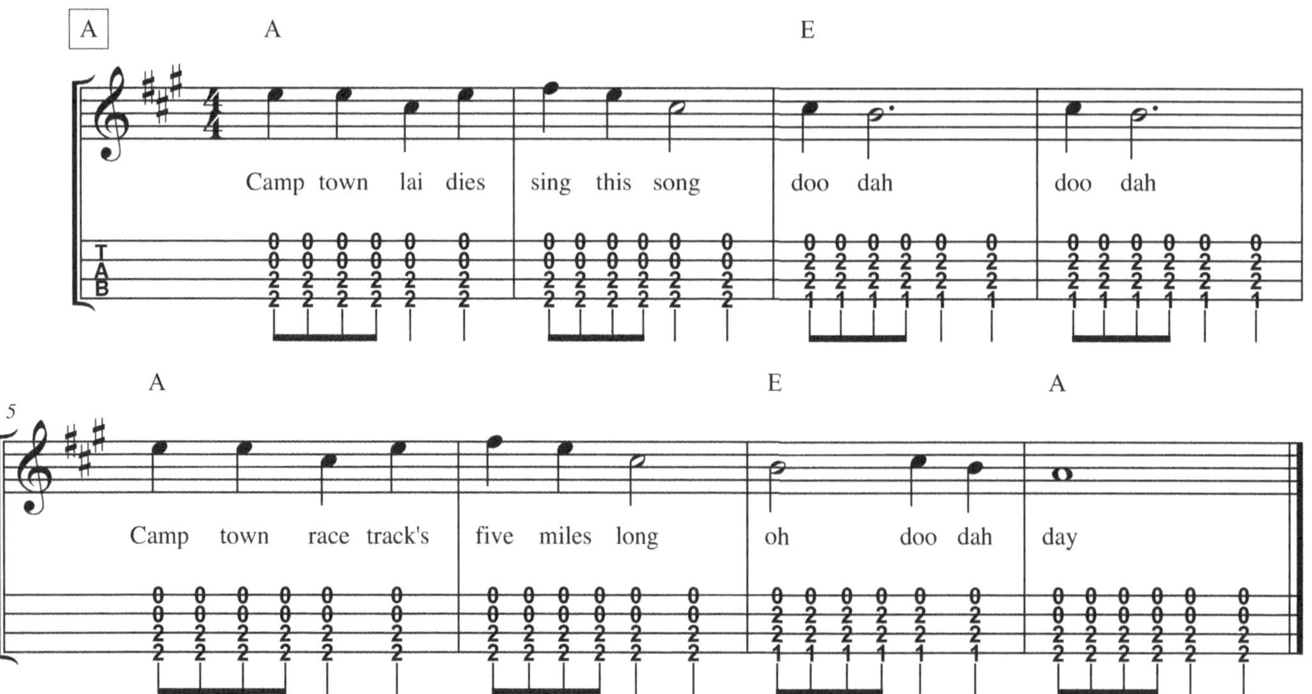

Use all of the rhythms above to vary your open chord rhythm however you'd like! You can practice along with the recording. Once you've mastered *Camptown Races,* learn to play open chords and rhythm to all of the tunes in the book!

Chop Chords and Rhythm

Bluegrass and swing mandolin players use a percussive rhythm technique called "chops." They use "closed" position chords (no open strings) so the sustain of the chord can be made very short and percussive rather than long and ringing as in open chords.

Below are all of the chop chords for the tunes in this book. Some of these chords require challenging finger stretches. They are difficult at first and may be fatiguing. Practice them frequently for short intervals and your left hand will develop muscle memory, strength and speed. Gradually they will become much easier.

Chop Chords

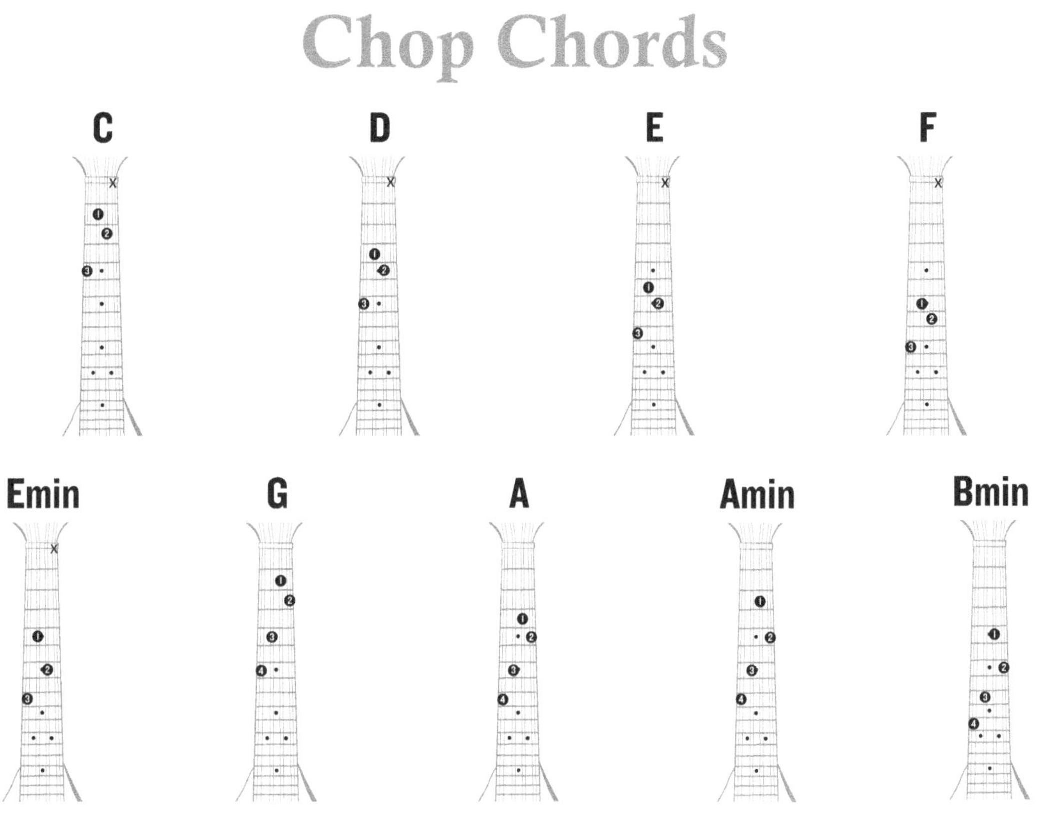

x = don't play that string

Note that because there are no open strings, these patterns are completely movable. For example, if you move the A chord up one fret (towards the bridge), it becomes a B♭ (A♯) chord. If you move it up one more fret more it becomes a B. Likewise, if you shift the D up one fret it's an E♭ (D♯), and if you move it up one more fret it's an E. *By moving the closed positions up and down the neck, you can play any major or minor chord!*

Chop rhythm is played on beats 2 and 4. These are called "backbeats" (beats 1 and 3 are the "downbeats"). Though you won't chop on beats 1 and 3, many mandolin players keep time by making a "ghost strum" on those beats. They may even touch down lightly on the G string. This can help to keep your right hand moving on all four beats like a metronome.

The distinctive chop rhythm sound is crisp and short rather than rich and sustained as it is in the open chord sound. Comparing open chord and chop chord sounds to a drum kit, the open chord is like a cymbal with a long sustained ring and the chop chord is like a snare with a "thwap!" sound.

To make this sound, strum through the strings fairly aggressively, but a split second after the chord sounds, relax the fingers of your left hand to kill the strings' sustain. Don't lift your fingers off the strings but just relax them enough to mute the string vibration. It takes a bit of practice to coordinate the precise timing of your right and left hands. Listen to the recording and copy the sound of the chop rhythm.

(Tip: Beginners often play chops too loudly! On a scale of 1–10, if 1 is as softly as you can play, and 10 is your loudest, shoot for chops at a 3 volume.)

Now play chop chords on beats two and four in Camptown Races.

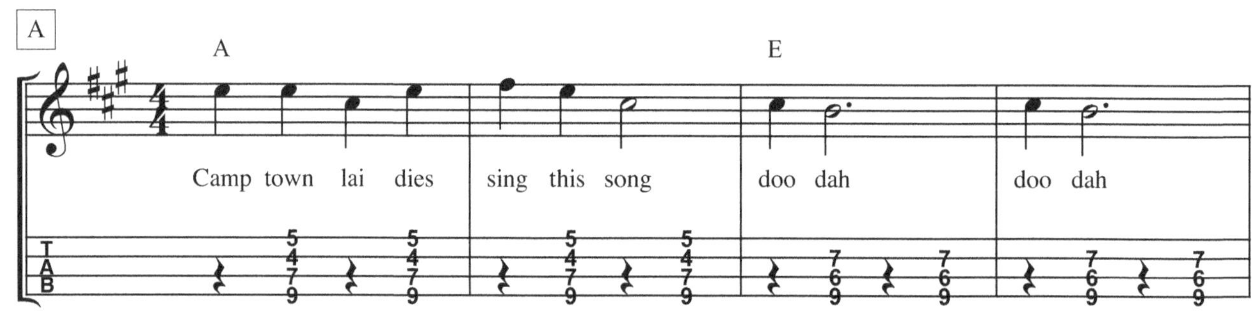

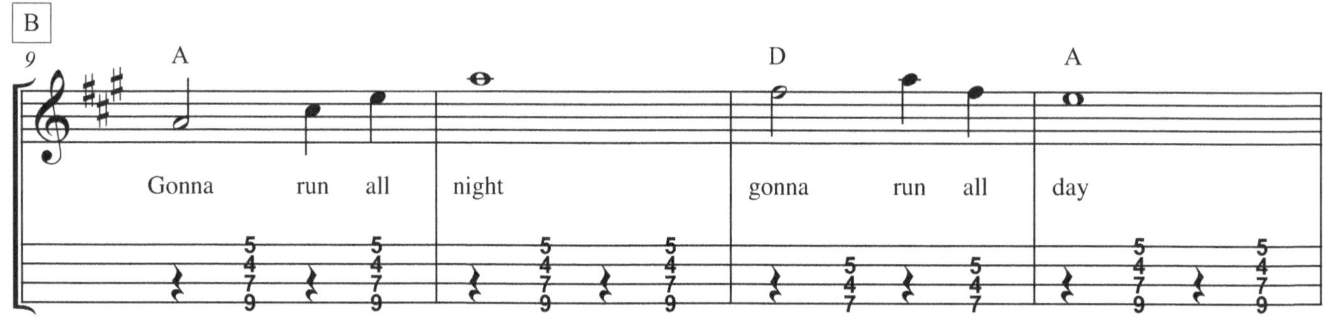

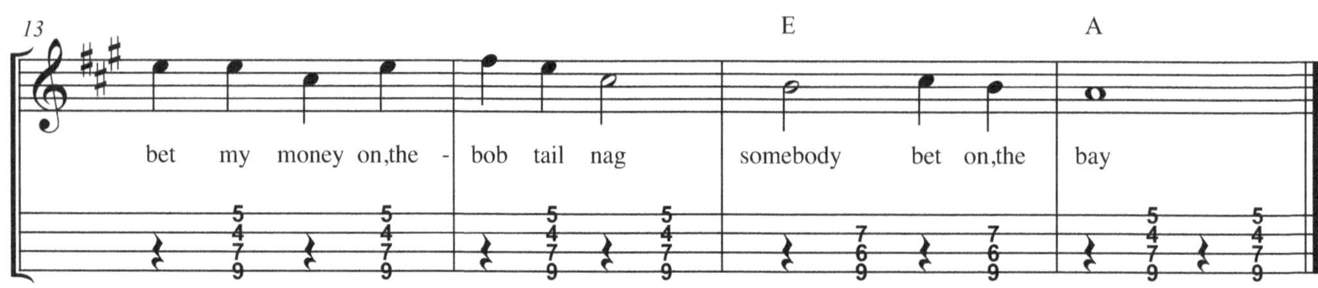

Chop Chords with Waltzes

A tune with three quarter note beats per measure (3/4) is a waltz. *Country Waltz*, *Amazing Grace*, *Down in the Valley*, *Aaran Boat Song*, *Si Beag Si Mor* and *Southwind* are all waltzes. Both open chords and chop chords sound great with these songs. Play chops with waltzes on beats two and three, leaving beat one for the guitar or bass.

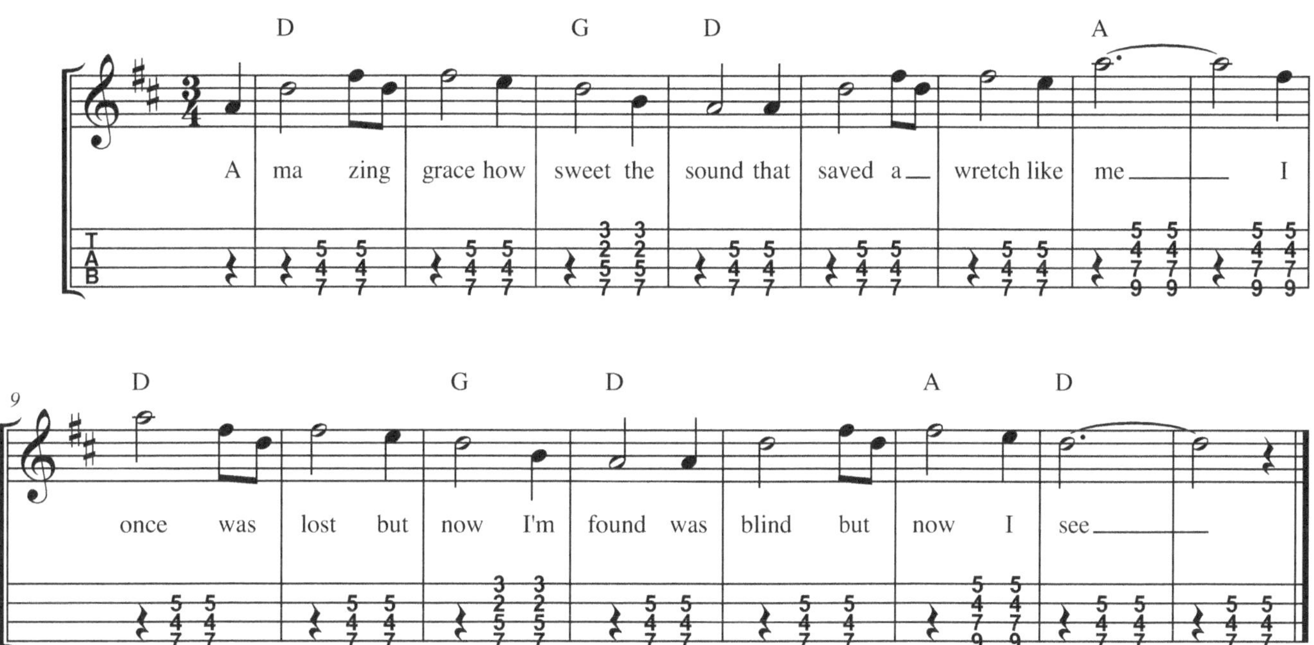

Review Chart

After you can play a tune without mistakes, write down the date. Do a review session every few months to keep your repertoire fresh and ready to go. Don't forget the chords and any variations. If you do a good job reviewing, you'll remember the tunes forever!

		Date	Date	Date
1	Boil 'em Cabbage Down			
2	Shortnin' Bread			
3	Little Liza Jane			
4	Camptown Races			
5	Cripple Creek			
6	Buffalo Gals			
7	Angelina Baker			
8	Old Joe Clark			
9	Cindy			
10	Crawdad Song			
11	Bonaparte's Retreat			
12	Red Haired Boy			
13	Country Waltz			
14	Girl I Left Behind Me			
15	Down in the Valley			
16	Amazing Grace			
17	Red River Valley			
18	Shady Grove			
19	Sugar Hill			
20	Cluck Old Hen			
21	Arran Boat Song			
22	Over the Waterfall			
23	Si Beag Si Mor			
24	Sandy Boys			
25	Southwind			
26	Red Wing			
27	Cairo			
28	Miss McLeod's Reel			
29	Turkey in the Straw			
30	Stinky's Blues			

MEL BAY ®

Made in the USA
Columbia, SC
06 April 2026

81396051R00043